BASE CAMP

Caitlin Press Inc.
8100 Alderwood Road,
Halfmoon Bay, BC V0N 1Y1
www.caitlin-press.com

Edited by Jane Silcott.
Copy edit by Kathleen Fraser.
Text design by Vici Johnstone.
Cover design by Edmund Arceo of Spiderplus Graphics.
Map illustration by Sheryl McDougald.
All photos copyright Dianne Whelan unless otherwise noted.
Printed in Canada

Caitlin Press Inc. acknowledges financial support from the Government of Canada
through the Canada Book Fund and the Canada Council for the Arts, and from the
Province of British Columbia through the British Columbia Arts Council and the
Book Publisher's Tax Credit.

Library and Archives Canada Cataloguing in Publication

Whelan, Dianne, 1965-, author
       Base camp : 40 days on Everest / Dianne Whelan.

ISBN 978-1-927575-43-7 (bound)

       1. Whelan, Dianne, 1965- —Travel—Everest, Mount (China and Nepal).
2. Mountaineering—Everest, Mount (China and Nepal). 3. Everest, Mount
(China and Nepal)—Description and travel. 4. Everest, Mount (China and
Nepal)—Environmental conditions. I. Title.

GV199.44.E85W44 2014   796.522095496   C2013-908504-1

BASE CAMP
40 DAYS ON EVEREST

DIANNE WHELAN

CAITLIN PRESS

CONTENTS

To know a people you must spend forty days with them.
—Arabic proverb

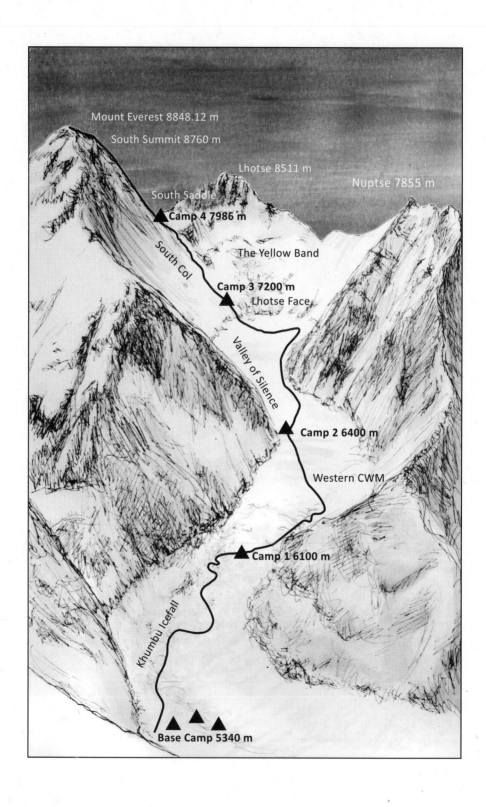

INTRODUCTION

This is not a story about getting to the top of Mt. Everest. This is a story about what happens halfway up, at a place called Base Camp. At 5,364 metres, cradled in million-year-old granite, Base Camp is a barren waste-land incapable of sustaining life. Nothing grows there. It is not a place you would expect anybody to put up a tent, but every spring thousands do.

I got my first chance to go there in 2007, when I was hired by *Outpost* magazine to write a feature article about making the 92-kilometre trek to Base Camp. I was excited to go to the holy mecca of mountaineers, the mythic realm of Hillary and Tenzing. Ever since I was a child I've been fascinated by the story of their first summit. There was something noble about it, a man from the east and a man from the west together achieving what was thought impossible, the dream that had already killed many of those who had tried. What I liked best: they never admitted who stood on top first.

It was a grey and cold day in late May when I arrived for that first visit. The camp consisted of hundreds of yellow, red, blue and green tents scattered across acres of ice and moraine. There was no even ground to stand on, and everywhere I looked I was surrounded by dirty ice, dark rock, garbage and melting glacier water. This was far from the pristine mountain scene I'd expected; rather, it looked more like a temporary camp of refugees in a barren and inhospitable place. Nothing lives or grows at 5,300 metres. Nothing grows in the ground. There is only 50 percent as much oxygen in the air as there is at sea level. So it was hard on my body, triggering headaches, insomnia, and crazy dreams. Then I met a guy who told me about some oxygen being stolen from Camp Four. At this point my noble myth died. I was glad to leave after a few hours, and remarked to one of the women I was trekking with, "I guess I can cross that off the bucket list, tick, no need to go back there again."

But for months after I returned I couldn't stop thinking about it: the ego, the selfishness, the garbage and the desecration of nature. I wanted to make a film about it.

So I returned in April 2010, this time to spend forty days on Everest filming an independent documentary called *40 Days at Base Camp.*

It takes a climber about forty days to climb Everest. In part that was why I decided to spend that amount of time at Base Camp, but I was also thinking of the symbolic meaning that forty days has in just about every religion in the world as a period of self-reflection.

I read recently that we are not defined by what we want because we all want money, health, love and happiness. We are defined by what we are willing to suffer for, and I was willing to suffer to make this film.

I admit in the final days leading up to my departure, I got a bad feeling. The wheels were in motion, the financing and equipment were in place to go, tickets booked, so there was no turning back. But deep down, beneath my confident exterior, I was scared. I knew spending forty days on Everest was going to change my life. And it did.

This is the story of forty days at Base Camp.

KATHMANDU

Our party of three arrives in Kathmandu from Canada late at night after thirty-two hours of travel with 900 pounds of gear in thirteen duffel bags. A red half moon in a black sky greets our arrival. It's good to arrive here late at night when the chaos of Kathmandu is sleeping. On empty streets we are ten minutes from our hotel, a journey that by day could easily take well over an hour.

At the hotel, there is strong coffee and fruit and eggs in a large dining room where the floor staff outnumber the handful of white guests. Hotel Shanker was once a palace when Nepal was a Hindu monarchy. That ended in 1990. Now, shadows of that greatness linger in the grey marble floors, the creamy clay arches, the glass chandeliers and the pillars painted with golden dragons with elephant heads and snake tongues. Dying myths are everywhere.

The gardens are well groomed, full of fuchsias and miniature palm trees, and this morning the air is fresh after the rain that washed away yesterday's dust and smog. We will spend three days in Kathmandu. At 1,400 metres, this is our first step in acclimatizing to higher altitudes as all three of us live at sea level back home.

Andrew Coppin is my director of photography. He is a kind and genuine man. He is thirty-two and fit, doesn't drink or smoke, and is what I call a technical cameraman. He likes technology, takes the time to understand it, and is methodical and disciplined. He was raised by a family of nuclear scientists and is an atheist. I saw a film he shot and liked his eye. And he had just spent six years working on *The L Word* as a camera assistant: all good signs. But it was for his left brain that I hired him. I am a very intuitive photographer and filmmaker. I smoke and drink. I was raised in a Catholic family and I read my horoscope faithfully. I don't have an aptitude for the science and math, but I have the feel for a good shot. So my right brain was looking for a left brain to bring on the journey. I found it in Andrew.

Teresa is my partner. We have been together for ten years. She is kind and generally calm, has beautiful blue eyes, and is the quintessential embodiment of the word *yin*. She has made the world slow down for me, made my house a home, and the simple moments of pleasure more seductive than the big adventures. With her, I have stayed still longer than I ever have in my life. She will travel with Andrew and me for the first two weeks of the trip, hike the beginning of the trail, then fly home to British Columbia as Andrew and I push on to Base Camp.

After breakfast we go to the lobby to meet Bashista, the Nepalese government representative who will travel with Andrew and me, at my expense, for the entire trip. This is not something I am happy about. Bringing Bashista will cost me ten thousand dollars. To a documentary filmmaker, the idea of it feels Orwellian. As I approach him he reaches out his hand and gives me his business card. Printed on thin white paper, it reads: Bashista P. Adhikari, Ministry of Information & Communications. He looks to be in his late fifties and has thick eyebrows and dark eyes. He is Hindu and, I am guessing, like most Hindu men of his generation in this culture, probably thinks women are inferior. A girl is to be governed by her father, a married woman by her husband. I am not docile or obedient. I know intuitively this is going to be challenging. I introduce him to Teresa and Andrew and we make a plan to meet the following morning to do some filming in Kathmandu.

After a morning spent testing the equipment we set out in the late afternoon to the offices of Asian Trekking, whom I have hired to help with permits, equipment and logistics. Although we are in Kathmandu quite literally to catch our breath, as soon as I step outside the gates of the hotel, the pace of the city makes me breathless. It's like a beehive on acid. It's a fifteen-minute walk from the gated oasis of the Hotel Shanker into an area called Thamel, where the narrow streets are crowded with vendors, three-wheeler rickshaws called tuk tuks, motorcycles and cars. After a few minutes I see there is a beauty to the chaos, and I don't miss the corporate logos, or large chain stores. Here there are many small shops, the constant beeping of horns, idling engines and somehow, in the din of it all, birds chirping. This is a city of 1.7 million with a crumbling infrastructure, a weak government and constant blackouts because there just isn't enough power. The hotels have generators that kick in when the power goes out, which happens eighty hours a week. Most locals have flashlights and candles. Water is delivered in big trucks because the city's water pipes are leaking and contaminated. And the show goes on. Charles Darwin was right—those who survive must learn to adapt.

As well as everything else there are protests and political unrest; angry young men dressed in green army fatigues march down streets. In the hotel lobby, I'd heard there was a threat of a Mao rebellion shutting down the government offices—not something you want to hear when you are spending your life savings on an indie film.

ASIAN TREKKING

As we step off the busy streets into the Asian Trekking office we go from car gridlock and Mao rebels to a large open room where a group of young children laugh as they scramble up a climbing wall looking for hand holds.

Of more than thirty expedition companies that take people to Everest, I chose this company because the owners of Asian Trekking are a Sherpa family and one of the biggest expedition companies in Nepal and Tibet. They handle all the government paperwork and Base Camp logistics. Ang Tshering started the company in 1982 and now runs it with his son, Dawa Steven. This year Dawa Steven will be at Base Camp to oversee nine clients who have hired Asian Trekking to guide them to the summit. His father, Ang, will stay in Kathmandu.

Ang Tshering wears a shirt and tie. He has built a very successful company and is able to provide seasonal jobs to hundreds of people. His son, Dawa, went to university in Scotland, speaks impeccable English, is young, handsome and well-spoken, cares about the environment and his culture, and could be a future leader of this country. Knowing I will be spending time with Dawa at Base Camp, I focus the interview on Ang and begin by asking how his family got to be involved in the climbing industry. He tells me that his great-great-grandfather was involved in the first Everest expedition of 1921 and was also with the 1924 expedition when George Mallory and Andrew "Sandy" Irvine attempted to summit. "So we have a very long history of mountain-living background," he says, explaining that the Sherpa people who came from Eastern Tibet over five hundred years ago used to cross Lola Pass, which is over 6,000 metres high. "But at that time nobody cared, nobody noticed. The Sherpa people, when they go to Tibet, crossed very high passes with simple shoes, simple clothing.

Sherpas have always climbed. My grandfather died when I was a baby but my father had a lot of these stories to tell. Even when I was a young kid, I was curious what is behind the Himalayas. When the foreigners came, they looked very white compared to the Sherpa people. And my parents, my grandparents, they used to say the foreigners were made from butter."

This makes me laugh. Our western privileges certainly make us comfortable, and perhaps also weaker. Ang Tshering was a small child when Hillary and Tenzing climbed Everest in 1953. At that time the Sherpa people in Nepal had no schools and no medical facilities. Until 1950 Nepal was closed off to the world. But that all changed after Hillary and Tenzing climbed Everest. It was the beginning of development in Khumbu. While Ang's father was travelling with Hillary in the 1960s Hillary asked what he could do for the Sherpas, and Ang's father said, "We have eyes but we cannot see, ears but we cannot hear. We need schools for our children."

So in 1960 Hillary went to Khunde and built the first Sir Edmund Hillary School for the Sherpa children. Ang was one of the first students, and Asian Trekking was the first company to take people on guided expeditions to the top.

Our conversation drifts to how things have changed. Ang says there have been a lot of technological changes since the time of Mallory and Irvine, but there have also been many environmental changes, and the climbing has become harder because the glaciers have melted and exposed more rock. In addition, glacial lakes have emerged. "One example I like to give in the Everest area is Imja Glacier," he says, "one of the most potentially dangerous outbursts of a glacial lake. I remember very well in 1960 the Imja Lake did not exist at all. In 1962 it appeared as a small pond. And in 2008 a scientist group from Japan measured the lake and it was 2.3 kilometres long, 900 metres wide, 92 metres deep. We were very afraid after they told us the measurements. It is just in front of Everest, and Everest is our tourism basket. If this lake outbursts it will create a vertical tsunami. It will wash away all the properties, and generations of families will be washed away." Ang looks at me seriously. "The sea level is rising because of excessive melting of glaciers, so [there are] a lot of relations between the mountain and sea. We are worried because of climate change, because of the global warming and the GLOF, which means the glacier lake outbursts. These are a global problem. But the poor mountain community, they have to face the problem. They have to pay the prices even though they are not guilty of climate change."

After our meeting, Andrew, Teresa and I walk back through the busy streets of Kathmandu to slip behind the gates to the expansive lawns of the Hotel Shanker. As Ang was speaking of the climate change on Everest and in the Himalayas, it occurred to me that I had heard a very similar story from the Inuit in the Canadian Arctic. Like the Sherpas, they too are suffering from the consequences of melting ice from global warming despite not having contributed to the causes. This realization gives new meaning to what Ang said about the connection between the mountain and the sea.

ANI CHOYING

Before a climber tries to climb Mt. Everest, it is customary for him or her to go to a monastery along the way for a blessing by a Buddhist monk. In 2007 my Sherpa guide, Pasang, took the trekking group I was with to three monasteries for blessings en route. At the first two I sat quietly and respectfully, soaking up all the ritual and chanting. During the last one we had tea with a monk, and I asked him when he thought women might be monks. After a raised eyebrow I got a chuckle and the response, "Not for a long time."

This trip I decided to do things differently. I would still pay my respects at the monasteries but I would also go to a convent. This led me to Ani Choying Drolma, a well-respected Buddhist nun and singer living in Nepal. I had read that she ran away from an abusive father at the age of thirteen and found a home in a convent, where there happened to be a master Buddhist chanter. He taught her how to sing. Ani Choying has gone on to release albums that sit on top of the charts in Nepal. She performs around the world and gives the proceeds from her music to a non-profit organization she created called the Nuns Welfare Foundation of Nepal. The organization funds various projects for runaway and orphaned girls, elderly women and stray dogs.

At the door of her convent I am greeted by the half-dozen fourteen-year-old girls who run the Ani Choying empire. I buy six of Ani's different CDs and one of the girls leads us to a room in the basement. Minutes later Ani walks in wearing a deep orange cashmere shawl over a black t-shirt and black skirt, her head shaven. She radiates the calm of a person who has found her purpose in life. We sit down and begin our discussion. I tell her that I am humbled by how one person could have the vision and the ability to help so many women.

"I give whatever I can to give real proper meaning to my existence in this world," she begins. "Somehow, music has been the key to [doing] what I want to do. When I tour I make money from CDs and people pay for the tickets, and when I come back, that's a lot of money. So I have the freedom and financial resources. Of course it's human nature, the more you have the more you want. I wish sometimes I had a magic wand and anyone I see in trouble I could just..." She smiles, waving her imaginary wand. We talk about some of her new projects and I am impressed with her insight, compassion and eloquence. She asks me what my film on Everest is going to be about.

"I am not sure," I say. "It will be a direct cinema film, an observation of a place. I will search for story, not impose it. But philosophically, I am curious to know, if you commercialize the sacred, does it lose its meaning? What do you think about all of the garbage and human excrement spread over a mountain that many people see as a goddess?"

"I do not think this is intentional. It is ignorance," Ani responds. "When you get things for free you seem to take it for granted. For instance, the air—air is the most important thing for us to survive. We don't see it; we just have it, you know, so we don't really think about it that much."

I share with Ani that I was raised in a Catholic family and rebelled against it as a teenager. "I didn't come from the rib of a man, I came from the womb of a woman," I say, then ask if it bothers her that only men get to be monks in Buddhism.

Ani smiles. "That's how you see it from the outside, but that is not exactly how it is because I am in it myself. No Buddhist master comes and says, 'Here, you must respect me or you must bow down to me.' The first and foremost practice of the Buddhist practices is humbleness, respect—to be kind, to be thoughtful. But the very natural practice is also there. That is, when someone is more educated, more learned, or more senior, automatic respect is there. And as I said earlier, monks have been having good opportunities in academic education. And they are learned, and whether we like it or not, it is a very automatic thing that we respect that."

At this, her smile disappears. "We never go and say, 'You are educated but I am the same as you, I'm a woman, you're a man.' But then I'm not at the stage of rebelling and thinking, 'Oh they are doing everything, they are getting everything.' I am not angry about it. One of my favourite lines says, 'Instead of cursing the darkness, why not light a candle yourself?'

"Really. That's exactly what I believe. Rejoice in everything others have, but don't be angry about it. And if there is something that you want, then try to get it yourself. Don't expect anyone else to come and give it to you. In the end, [with] aggression, if it is negative, the first person that will be harmed is you, because you are not comfortable, in your mind, in your body."

Ani levels her gaze right at me. "And of course speech is not nice either, once you are full of anger. So over the years till now I have been able to learn these things and that has only been possible through the teachings of Buddha. I am blessed and I want to be able to share this with everyone. Whether that is through my singing, or my activities…"

"By example," I interject.

"I don't know if I can be an example that is for the others to do it," she says, smiling again. "I don't want to say that I am an example. I never do this myself to be an example. I want to do it myself to really be happy. And that has made me happy. When I am happy I am able to make others happy. When I see others happy, and that's when they probably want to find a way to be happy themselves, then probably they will adopt the way I do things. But I never say that you should do this or you should do that. People are intelligent enough, actually, the most intelligent creature in this world."

Laughing, she adds, "Probably."

DINNER WITH MEAGAN

We wrap up our last night in Kathmandu with dinner with a climber named Meagan McGrath, a forty-year-old Canadian who works for the Canadian Air Force and spends her off-duty time climbing the world's highest mountains. Meagan is going to be at Everest Base Camp to climb Lhotse, the 8,516-metre peak beside Everest. Meagan is one of Asian Trekking's clients and I am hoping she will be one of my characters in the documentary. Although this is the first time I have met her, our paths have crossed before.

On my way back to Canada after my first Everest visit in 2007, I had a stopover in London. I was quite sick, and as I lay in my hotel bed sweating and coughing and watching TV, a brief news spot came on CNN about Everest. The story centred on a Canadian climber who had saved the life of a Nepali woman who got into trouble near the summit. I used the story in my article to show there are still climbers who exemplify humanity and bravery in contemporary climbing, and I presented her story as a ray of hope in an otherwise dark article about the many climbers who leave others to die as they make their way to the summit.

Andrew, Teresa and I meet Meagan around the corner from our hotel at an oasis garden and restaurant behind a long, white brick wall. The manicured parts of Kathmandu are all behind walls. We have a lovely dinner and, knowing the hiking will begin the next day, enjoy decadent chocolate desserts. It is too dark to film and I know I wanted to record her telling the story of the rescue on Everest, so instead I ask her about her last trip, a solo cross-country ski trip to the South Pole. She mesmerizes us with a harrowing tale of falling into a crevasse on her second day of that trip. For eight hours she hung upside down, attached by a rope to the sled she was pulling, which acted as a bridge over the crevasse. She thought she was going to die at first, and felt bad for her mother. She was alone in the middle of a frozen world of Antarctic ice. "The ass kicker of that one is that I had an Iridium satellite phone," she tells us enthusiastically.

"We used them in the Arctic when I travelled with the military and Inuit up the north coast of Ellesmere Island," I say.

"Yes, use them in the Arctic because that's where they go. They don't really work that well everywhere else," she laughs. "I am sponsored by them. They are polar satellites. I tried to test mine in Ottawa, I tried to test it in Chile. I wasn't getting a signal, and I was like, 'Holy fuck, I'm bringing this thing to Antarctica and it is never going to work.' The second day in Antarctica, I am hanging upside down in a crevasse and I hold the thing up and it had five bars [of signal strength]. I was at the bottom of a crevasse and it worked. It saved my life."

I ask Meagan's advice about sending stuff forward with yaks when we get to Lukla. We have eleven bags, 400 kilograms of gear, and we only need to hike in with a few items of clothing and a camera. She advises us to send most of our gear ahead once we get to Lukla with the yaks and reassures us that our Sherpa guide can arrange that for us tomorrow. I tell her I have an entire duffel bag filled with a range of medications and lots of food: granola bars, beef jerky and fruit bars. "Andrew is skinny enough," I say. "We can't have him losing any weight up there."

"He will, though," Meagan says, explaining that some people lose their appetite at high-altitude.

When Andrew asks whether forcing down his food will allow him to maintain his weight, Meagan tells him, "You are skinny and you are going to lose weight and that is the way it is going to be."

I am encouraged by this piece of news, as I have been fattening up on chocolate cake as part of my training.

LUKLA

At 6 a.m., a driver and our government escort, Bashista, pick us up to take us to the airport. We are heading to Lukla, which at 2,860 metres is the starting point for most treks through the Himalayas to Mount Everest. After meeting Ani I have vowed to be kinder and more open-minded about Bashista. I know I met him with a negative attitude and want to try again with an open heart.

Our flight is supposed to leave at 7:30 a.m. but we are delayed because the air traffic control tower is suffering some equipment failure so they are directing planes manually. Visibility is also poor because a thick haze hangs over the city and runways. I kill time trying to read the directions written in tiny print on my bottle of acetazolamide (Diamox), a medication for altitude acclimatization. I have never liked taking pills. I generally smoke a joint for all that ails me. If it doesn't make me better, at least it always makes me *feel* better. But since my trip in 2007, I've known that my body would have difficulty acclimatizing to the higher altitudes. And altitude sickness, also known as acute mountain sickness (AMS), can kill you. When the body has not acclimatized to its current altitude, headaches, nausea, fatigue, dizziness and disturbed sleep, all symptoms of AMS, can occur in varying degrees, from mild to severe. At the severe end are high-altitude cerebral edema (HACE), a fancy name for fluid in the brain, and high-altitude pulmonary edema (HAPE), which is fluid in the lungs. The best cure for either is always immediate descent. Failure to do so results in death within twenty-four hours. According to the six-point font I'm trying to read, I should start taking the Diamox when I get to Lukla.

The haze lifts a bit as morning moves on and at 10 a.m. we are ready for takeoff. The plane is a twin-engine sixteen-seater with one seat on each side of the aisle. Our flight path weaves between the peaks of mountains. At times it appears the plane's wings are just a few metres from the mountain rock and terraced hillsides.

The woman sitting in front of me gets a nosebleed on our final approach into Lukla airport, which is just a small runway carved into a hillside. There's no room for error here. Overshoot the landing and the plane will burst into flames as it hits the mountain wall. A few of these planes crash every year. Hillary's first wife and daughter perished on one of these flights years ago, and the plane we're on today will crash in four months' time, killing both my pilots and the airline attendant.

But today the twenty-five-minute flight from Kathmandu lands safely at the Tenzing-Hillary airport and I breathe a sigh of relief as we step onto the tarmac of what's known as the most dangerous airport in the world.

Lukla means "where the sheep graze." But I see no sheep, only chickens running all over and dzokyos, the cow-yak hybrids used as pack animals to carry supplies. The idea is to spend two days filming and acclimatizing at this high-altitude location before we start the long hike toward Everest. We are greeted by our Sherpa guide, Childon, who it seems is good friends with Bashista. Childon helps us gather all our bags and navigate our way to our hotel, which, as it happens, is the first one we come across walking into town.

Paradise Lodge is run by Dawa Futi Sherpa, who was good friends with Hillary and one of the first girls to go to the school he built in the 1960s. Now she runs Lukla's primary trekkers' lodge, while her husband works at the airport. This is helpful here in Lukla where there can be a lot of bad weather days. Cloud, haze, and strong winds prevent the planes from landing or taking off, creating backlogs of people who need a place to stay, so it pays to have connections.

I find it interesting that here in Nepal men and women can have the same name. One of a Sherpa's names will always be the day of the week they were born. Dawa means Monday, and I will meet several Dawas over my time here. Dawa Futi Sherpa is in her fifties. She comes across as a confident, strong woman. Today she is wearing a striped dress with a pink cardigan and a pearl necklace and earrings. We are drinking tea inside her lodge, the interior of which is all varnished wood: walls, tables and benches. Hanging on the walls are pictures of her friend Sir Edmund Hillary. She pulls out two photo albums filled with pictures of Hillary's visits.

Dawa is originally from a small village called Khumjung, a few days' walk from here. She came to Lukla twenty years ago and has been running Paradise Lodge since then.

The Lukla airstrip was built by Hillary in 1964. He did not mean to build it for the trekkers, having no idea how many trekkers would actually come. Rather, he did it to build hospitals and to bring supplies. Consequently, Dawa has seen lots of changes. When she went to school in the 1960s she was one of only three girls who attended school. That is when she met Hillary. "My father always insisted I go to school," she explains. "Now each and every girl goes to school. In 1964 Hillary had to go door to door to beg them to send their children to school."

Dawa was twelve before she wore her first shoes. Now newborn babies get shoes and socks. She had never seen a telephone, and planes were strange, loud objects that just flew overhead. Now she has a cellphone and an Internet connection, and planes land right behind her lodge. She has also seen dramatic changes to the climate in Lukla. "Twenty years ago, there was lots of snow; this year, no snow. I have never seen mist like this before. I think this is because of climate change. We are very worried but there is nothing we can do. It is in the hands of everybody. We are a Third World country, we can't do anything."

Dawa's father worked with Hillary in 1953 and summited in 1965. He was killed in an avalanche on Everest in 1979. "Hillary liked us very much because there were many boys but only two [other] girls at the school," Dawa says, adding that she went to visit Hillary in New Zealand two months before his death. "We talked about the Himalayan Trust. We have sixty-three schools to look after." She shows us photo albums filled with her pictures of Hillary and talks of her love and admiration for the man. I am a bit awestruck that within hours of being on the trail to Everest, we're already one degree of separation from Edmund Hillary. If Everest is the heart, the trail is the main artery. Everybody here is woven into the history and story of Everest.

I ask Dawa what she thinks of all the development that has happened in Khumbu since Hillary built the airport.

"Deforestation, garbage, climate change, changes of the culture… these things are bad. Now it's about the oldest climber, the youngest climber. They don't respect the mountain. One day when the weather is good they all go up the mountain at once, like a street here. Everybody goes up there." Dawa raises her arm above her head. "Then they go home, 'I climb Everest, I climb Everest.' That's not the thing. They should just go there and look at it, experience the feelings of the mountain, then respect the mountain and then it is good, you know. The Sherpas have to carry all their stuff and drag them up the mountain so they can take their picture up there. 'I climb Everest, I climb Everest.' They do nothing for the mountain; they do nothing for the people. They are disrespectful to the mountains."

She pauses, looks at her hands. I'm thinking about asking her if she's read what Hillary said about being horrified by what has happened on Everest, but then Dawa looks up. Her voice is softer as she says there have also been good things like education and jobs. Her son is in Australia going to university, and she is running her own business. Then her cellphone rings, and the interview is over.

THE HIKE

After two days in Lukla, Andrew, Teresa, Bashista, Childon and I embark on the centuries-old trail that leads to Base Camp, part of which is the same trail Hillary and Tenzing walked all those years ago when they hiked to Khumbu all the way from Kathmandu.

The trail is like stepping back in time. The traditional stone paths are carved into the hillsides and are shared with locals, porters, yaks and dzo-kyos, as well as several other trekkers, some going just as far as Namche Bazaar, some also heading to Base Camp. People spread out and walk at their own pace. Here, the excessive rush of modernity disappears and life unfolds at the pace of a walk, with only the sound of yak bells, birds, a distant river and my heavy breathing as accompaniment.

This is the paradise that comes before the austere rock and ice awaiting us beyond the treeline at Everest Base Camp. It's amazing to me how thin the habitable part of our troposphere is. What seems so infinite looking up into the sky is actually a thin veil of the breathable air that makes life possible on this planet; we are walking up toward its outer edge.

They say the eyes are the gateway to the soul. Painted on the stone walls next to the path, several pairs of Tibetan eyes stare out at us. A man from Texas remarks, "It's like their own version of surveillance cameras." We pass through fields filled with potatoes and barley, crops that will look very different in two months' time. Everywhere the landscape is infused with symbols of the strong beliefs of the predominantly Buddhist Sherpa people: prayer flags, prayer bells, monasteries and prayer domes called chortens, which guard the spirits of the dead memorialized on tablets placed beneath them.

I'm not religious, but I am spiritual. I've brought three talismans on this journey. The first comes from a Cree friend, Delphine Snakeskin: sweetgrass, to cleanse my spirit, and some of her child's umbilical cord, dried and put into a small hand-sewn deerhide pouch. This is the gift of the maiden. The second gift comes from my mother: a medal of her patron saint, St. Theresa, which I have pinned to my sports bra over my heart for protection. And last, a small gemstone, the genius stone, given to me by my elderly friend Mary Freemancin, who placed it ceremoniously in my left hand for vision on this journey. This is the gift of the crone.

I have allowed twelve days to hike into Base Camp, including the two-day acclimatization rest in Lukla and three days in Namche to adapt to the next jump. That leaves seven days of solid hiking. Our first day of hiking leaving Lukla is difficult. Two days of nausea and a poor appetite have left me feeling depleted even before the hiking begins. To make matters worse, the trail is very dusty, as the area has not had much rain. Mix that dust with a lot of dzokyo excrement and you have air full of bacteria. The sun is hot, the air toxic and my stomach empty, making for a hard 13-kilometre hike to Monjo, our first stop.

I think back to Meagan's advice given over dinner in Kathmandu to "wear your buffs." Most of the Sherpas, porters and experienced trekkers are all wearing these cotton versions of the knitted neck warmers I used to wear skiing. They pull them over their mouths when the trail gets dusty. We are using bandanas, which are not as effective. The buffs have an elasticity to the edges, which creates a better seal.

Over dinner in Monjo five hours later, I casually ask Andrew if he has any health issues I should know about. I am thinking specifically about allergies to the painkillers and medications I have brought. It turns out Andrew does indeed have an allergy to a certain kind of penicillin, but more importantly he also has a heart defect. Apparently he was born with a backwards heart. Andrew doesn't seem concerned, but I hold that worry in the back of my mind for the rest of the trip.

The next day brings a steep and long hill climb to Namche Bazaar. We've been hiking for about an hour when we come upon some men in military uniforms stopping people on the trail. Bashista and Childon speak to the men in Nepali while Andrew and I discreetly shoot some footage. After they let us pass, Bashista tells us that because of the political unrest in Kathmandu the army is stepping up surveillance on the Khumbu trails. A few years ago, Maoists murdered some tourists on the trekking trails and lost some local support because it hurt the communities financially. Tourists don't like to go where they might be killed. Violence is bad for business.

At 3,440 metres, the hillside village of Namche is the centre of the Khumbu region. Brightly painted shutters frame the windows of ancient stone buildings in a village that dates back to the fourteenth century. I am starting to get excited despite not feeling well. I can now see Everest in the distance. Namche is the main trading centre for this region and the last major stop-off point in the Himalayas before the trek to Base Camp. It has a market every weekend. *Nam* means forest, *che* means place, so Namche means place of forest, which was true when Tibetan settlers arrived five hundred years ago. They found water, so they stopped. But the trees they chopped down for firewood didn't grow back, so now it's a place of dry, barren hills.

But the town is still beautiful, built at terraced levels in an enclave in the mountains. What's interesting about development here is that they don't alter the landscape when they build. They don't use backhoes and dynamite, so everything looks more organic. They use rock for the walls and tin for the roofs. And of course there are no roads, just cobblestone and dirt walking paths. These are towns built for people, not cars. In that way it is like going back in time to see how we existed before the invention of the automobile. It is fascinating how *right* it feels.

Our conversations with locals repeatedly return to the subject of climate change. Over and over I hear people comment on what I can see, that the peaks are rock, that there has been no snowfall. They used to have three months of snow in winter, but now there is no snow. They all know they didn't cause it, and they have no way of expressing their anger. Their potatoes are in dry fields and they are praying for rain.

In Namche we stay at the Panorama Lodge, where I stayed three years ago. The lodge has Mars chocolate bars and a satellite Internet connection alongside primitive wood heating, Sherpas and yaks—a place caught between yesterday and tomorrow. In the West it seems we build our present on top of the ruins of the past. In Nepal, the past and present coexist side by side.

In the evening I get a brief lesson in Sherpa history from Sherab Jangbu, the patriarch of the family that runs the place. Many people in the West think Sherpa means "Guy who carries my bags up the mountain." It does not, as Jangbu explains.

"Sherpa is a clan, not an occupation. Sherpa means 'People from the east.' Our ancestors came from the far east of Tibet five hundred years ago. They lived on farming and later on trading with Tibet. In the 1920s some Sherpas went to Darjeeling for the cash flow because during that time there was a lot of construction there by the British government and that's how they were introduced to mountaineering. The British used them on the east side of Everest in the 1920s. Since then Sherpas have been introduced to mountaineering, and then later on the mountaineering started from India, then later in 1953–54 they started from Kathmandu. [In] 1953 when Sir Edmund Hillary climbed Everest, he started building schools for the Sherpa people. That opened the Sherpas' life much better, and since the 1970s trekking started in Nepal. So the economy of the Sherpas got better. Now Sherpas are not only climbing as an occupation: they are doctors, pilots, engineers. Many have their own businesses. The tourism in Nepal has helped a lot for the Sherpa people."

I ask Jangbu if he has any concerns, if there are any negative consequences to all the development.

"Now, because of the education, we are trying to send our kids to Kathmandu and then to America, but it is hard to bring them back," Jangbu says, shrugging. "But the main concern is the global warming. The glaciers are melting, that's a big problem. I do not know what is causing this, maybe the pollution from the cars, all the factories. I heard that the pollution down there is on top of Everest too."

We spend three days in Namche to acclimatize and to shoot some interviews. The break also gives me some time to start taking medication to combat the nausea I've been feeling for several days. Our room has hot showers, the last ones I'll see for fifty days. And the lodge has Internet access, our last affordable opportunity to send an email.

Luckily for me and my bad belly, the owners' daughter Rhita is a nurse with her own medical centre in Namche. She has a beautiful smile and looks much more Western than her parents, wearing a light blue Adidas jacket, t-shirt and jeans. Rhita has a machine to measure the oxygen level in the body. She clips a small black box with a red digital readout on the front onto my middle finger. My blood oxygen level is 93, and my pulse rate is 115, which is high. The most important thing to do, I am told, is to hydrate myself. She recommends I mix a pack of electrolytes into my water, at least 3 litres a day. Because of the dust and the dzokyo dung the air is inflammatory, bringing bacterial problems, which is what she thinks I have contracted. She gives me antibiotics and sends me on my way.

The next day, we visit Deedee, owner of a lodge in Namche. Bashista set up the interview for us. My initial resentment over having him along is mellowing now that I see him helping us meet locals.

Like the others we have met, Deedee speaks about climate change. "January was warm, no snow," she says. "It's a problem because no rain, bad for the potatoes. Very dry, lots of sickness, cough, fever. Because of the large cities, makes me angry, our government tries many times but not successful. I think it's not good to climb the mountain. To see the mountain is good but to climb is not good for the mountain. Lost many friends and Sherpas. One of our sisters died—she climbed most of the 8,000-metre mountains, and a few years ago she died on Lhotse."

I can see the strain behind her kind face, and I realize that the day her sister died in 2007, I was hiking down the trail from Base Camp. My Sherpa guide Pasang heard that a local woman had fallen. I remember being amazed at how he was able to learn what was happening on the mountain by exchanging information with people on the trail. We were a few days' hike from the mountain but news of her death had travelled 100 kilometres in under an hour. Her climbing rope had been cut by a jagged rock and she plummeted to her death.

Tonight the wind blows hard. At one point it sounds like a mountain falling down. Locals will tell me it is a dragon, their word for thunder. The next morning Teresa and I wake to the sound of a monk at a nearby monastery blowing into a conch shell. We are told the monks are praying for rain. Later that day, the rain arrives.

FINAL PUSH TO BASE CAMP

From Namche we hike uphill a few hours to Khumjung, where we do some filming at the first school Hillary built—the one both Ang and Dawa attended as children in the 1960s. In the middle of the school's courtyard a huge statue of Hillary honours his contribution to the Sherpa people and forever immortalizes the man who, for many, represents the true spirit of mountaineering. We interview the headmaster and drop off a gift from Canada—a fax machine. The headmaster is very grateful. This year they have eighteen teachers and three hundred students, seventy of whom stay here and are provided with food and lodging. He has been the head teacher for eleven years.

"When Hillary and Tenzing climbed Everest on May 29, 1953, they did so with the help of many Sherpas from the Khumbu region. That's why he wanted to give back to the Sherpas. This was the first school built in 1960 with just one building," he explains. This first building stands out amongst the area's many stone buildings as it is built from sheet metal, all of which was carried in on the backs of Sherpas from the airport Hillary built. The headmaster proudly shows us the library and the living quarters for students, who stay here because their villages are too far to walk back and forth to every day, all built with money raised by the Himalayan Trust started by Hillary. Up to seventy students can board here but he wants to build a big dining room and kitchen where one hundred students can sit and eat. The school now has many buildings, including a wooden one built by the Swiss, who shipped out the supplies and assembled it here. There are also cooks who make meals for the children from food paid for by the families. Textbooks and supplies like pencils and paper are paid for by the Himalayan Trust, which now also offers scholarships for students to go to university. It is impressive to see how the good intentions of one man have helped and inspired so many.

The next item on the agenda is to check out all our tents for Base Camp. This is where Asian Trekking stores equipment between climbing seasons. We will have a kitchen tent, a dining/office tent and small one-man tents for Andrew, me, Childon and Bashista. All of the equipment needs to be tested to ensure we don't leave without essential parts. Stoves, fuel lines, solar panels—everything is checked. Afterwards it is all neatly packed up. Childon's wife shows up with a small herd of yaks. We load up the gear and send it off a day ahead of us to get to Base Camp.

Tomorrow morning we all leave. Teresa will turn around and hike back to Lukla, and Andrew, Bashista, Sherpa Childon, our cook, Miloh, and I will embark on a long hike to Tengboche where there is a large monastery, the spiritual hub of the Khumbu region. We have permission to film there, and then we will push on to hike every day to Base Camp.

It will be close to two months before I see Teresa again. These separations are hard on our relationship. Sharing the first two weeks of the journey was meant to ease that strain but with the weight of the film on my mind it hasn't worked for me. I am anxious to get to Base Camp and worried about money. While she relaxes and plays games in the evenings with the crew, I download footage and make long lists of all the tasks before me. Teresa supports my ambition but wisely never chooses to put this kind of stress on herself. And as much as I respect that in her, I also resent it. And as much as I am sad to see her go, I am also relieved.

Along with this personal stress, I realize I've underestimated what will be required financially. We are not even 10 percent of the way through this trip and I have already spent 70 percent of the money. The biggest oversight was not factoring in the tipping for Sherpas, porters and cooks on a journey this long. Also, Internet expenses are high. The last time I was here there was no Internet past Namche. This year they have it all the way to Base Camp, but at a cost of one dollar a minute. It seems petty on a $70,000 production budget, but almost all of that was spent before we even hit the trail on permits, trekking company expenses, flights, insurance and equipment.

During the night I dream of a tarot card, the Princess of Wands. Every tarot card has a light and a shadow. The Princess of Wands is the body of a woman shaped like a flame. In the light the card represents passion, creativity and joy. In the shadow it represents arrogance and egocentricity. Hillary said, "We don't conquer the mountain, we conquer ourselves." The next morning as I stand crying with Andrew and the others as I watch Teresa walk back toward Lukla to head home, that is the battle I'm afraid of losing.

APRIL 17, 2010

The next morning I am eager to get to Base Camp as the climbers arrive. With Teresa gone, I decide to speed up our journey. Our hike begins with a descent into a river valley and across a new wire suspension bridge, then up a slow and steady climb to Tengboche Monastery, about 300 vertical metres today. I'm starting to get my legs back and, slowly, my lungs. I watch porters carry sixteen two-by-fours on their backs up the hill, while others carry three sheets of plywood each. Our porters are carrying the HVX500 (our large camera), the pelican case with hard drives, and the backpack with the Canon 5D and accessories, including the tripod. I have a small camel backpack with a small first aid kit, an extra water bottle, a light shell and wool pullover. And I'm huffing.

En route to Tengboche we bump into people on the trail coming back from their trek to Base Camp who tell us the camp has everything from an art exhibit on climate change with photos of the retreating glacier to a yoga tent sponsored by a long-underwear company. While building the landing pad for the helicopter, people found a detached human hand, with no clues as to which dead body it came from. I know I'm heading into a strange place—a kind of Burning Man of the Himalayas, only without the costumes and with darker undertones. Different fairytales, I guess.

Most people who try to summit Everest do so in April and May, before the monsoon season begins. They are all looking for that one perfect day, when the sky is clear and there is no wind at the top. That "weather window" varies from season to season. Some climbing seasons see a few of those days, some see none.

As I struggle up the final steep hill climb to Tengboche, my mind goes to the most common question people ask about climbing Everest: Why do it? Hiking higher and leaving all that is alive and growing behind, I can feel the air becoming thinner and ask myself the same question. What am I doing leaving what is comfortable and known for what will be painful and lonely? There are all sorts of things that can kill you on a trek like this. My heart is beating like it's wired on Red Bull—a heart attack comes to mind. And there are avalanches, crevasses, running out of oxygen, altitude sickness, being left to die. I've heard there are 250 dead bodies between Base Camp and the summit. Climbers have to hike through a graveyard of frozen dreams as they try to achieve their own. In some cases, a climber may have to literally step over the dead to get to the top. So, why, indeed? As Ang said in Kathmandu, Sherpas climbed passes over 6,000 metres high for centuries and nobody cared until 1856 when Everest was determined to be the highest peak in the Himalayas. Then the British cared very much about being the first to the top.

This is really a story about ambition. The ambition of those who want to tell their friends they climbed the highest mountain in the world, and my ambition to make this film. Ambition can be a good thing, but out of balance it can be destructive.

I find Tengboche shrouded in a cloud of mist. Andrew is already waiting for me at the lodge. Every guest lodge has the same basic design but they are on a sliding scale of cleanliness and decoration. Chances are if a Sherpa woman is in charge, the place will be more homey and clean. The lodging where we are staying in Tengboche doesn't appear to have any feminine touches, the only decoration a large black and white newsprint photo of Gandhi stuck to the stained plywood wall with clear tape. Which is cool in a bachelor kind of way. The region's traditional candle lanterns have been replaced with energy-efficient bulbs, their stark white fluorescent lighting giving a much colder ambiance than the candle lanterns.

Andrew and I order some food and settle in. I have had to pee for hours but as we have climbed higher the toilets have slid down in quality and now they are just smelly holes in the ground in some courtyard. Nothing makes a person confront the sensibilities of her Western culture more starkly than a bad outhouse. I am still drinking mint tea, which is foolish when I have to pee, but it gives me something warm to hold onto. I devise a plan to put some essential oil on a kerchief to wear to the rudimentary latrine.

In the dining room someone has lit a welcome fire of dried yak dung. Over two billion people use animal dung as an energy source; surprisingly, dried dung doesn't smell when burned. But the young man tossing the dung into the fire with his hands is also the guy cooking in the back, and I'm guessing he probably isn't washing them between duties. A few Sherpas are playing cards and my porters are sitting quietly enjoying the warmer room, as the weather is chilly outside. Tengboche is in a cloud and visibility is reduced to maybe a hundred metres. The mood is somber, altogether different from when the sun is shining.

Now every group is playing cards: a French group, a Sherpa/porter group and a German group. The room has a bench seat with carpets and pillows that runs along the walls, as well as wooden tables and an assortment of plastic patio chairs. For 550 rupees you can have a Heineken or a Tuborg. I want to but I don't. I venture to the latrine with my kerchief on my face. I feel like such a priss. But hey, that's what being soft like butter will do for you.

APRIL 18

I wake up early to film in Tengboche Monastery. Despite having obtained permission months ago, confirmed by Bashista and Childon when they talked to one of the monks just yesterday, we are told that they want three hundred dollars to let us film in the monastery. Is Tengboche Monastery going the direction of Rome? It doesn't sound like much, but in a place with no bank machines, I'm left with the money I have and again I am kicking myself for not bringing more. So we shoot some exteriors of the monastery in morning light and hit the trail. Childon suggests we film at another monastery a day's hike away in Pangboche.

Pangboche is also the village Childon is from. So we hike there and film the monks praying for another Sherpa from their community who is attempting to summit Everest this season. Pangboche Monastery is a more modest monastery than Tengboche. It's more than six hundred years old, and at 3,990 metres above sea level, it is one of the highest monasteries in the world. When Hillary and Tenzing summited, they went there for a blessing beforehand, so now many climbers follow the tradition. After filming the monks chanting and praying, we drink tea at Childon's home and then hike to Dingboche. We are two days from Base Camp. The terrain is arid and we are above the treeline—only short juniper shrubs and lichen grow here. We are entering a monochromatic landscape.

APRIL 19

It is a long day of hiking and filming under clear skies with stunning vistas. One of the porters is suffering from the high-altitude. I have a slight headache. We make a gain of 600 metres, putting us at nearly 5,000 metres. We hike to the Everest graveyard in Lobuche and do some filming at the Everest memorial site where dead bodies are brought and sometimes burned, if they can be recovered. We have not seen a tree for days. To burn a body here means carrying wood up from lower in the valley. The locals call on the lamas to come up to pray for the dead as their bodies return to dust. It is a sobering thought. The graveyard is filled with dozens of rock cairns, handmade tombstones for those who died in pursuit of their quest to stand on the top of the world. Many of these cairns are for Sherpas who died while taking people to the top. Dangerous job. One minute I am filled with awe, looking at the vista of all these beautiful Himalayan peaks set against a blue sky. The next minute, I am brought down to earth by the cairns of the dead. Childon kindly tells me he will burn my body here should I die while making my film. Comforting, sort of.

Our sick porter is still not well, and the last thing I want is for him to wind up in Lobuche permanently. I tip him and send him down to lower altitudes. We are now down to one porter and Sherpa for Base Camp. I pop an Advil, then, minutes later, pop two more.

BASE CAMP

DAY 1: APRIL 20

We arrive at Base Camp four days ahead of schedule, and already it is a sprawling tent city. It takes a full forty-five minutes just to walk through camp to find Asian Trekking. As one of the oldest expedition companies, they have one of the best locations, right at the base of the Khumbu Glacier. En route, I pass an unconscious white woman being carried out on a Sherpa's back and another white woman looking distressed, carrying her small baby wrapped in a blanket and sling. I wonder, how does a baby tell you if it has HAPE or HACE? Why would anyone bring a newborn almost three-quarters of the way up the world's highest mountain?

Base Camp is the end of the road. We are surrounded by some of the largest mountain peaks in the world: Pimouri, Lhotse, Nuptse and numerous other peaks I have yet to put names to. You can't see the peak of Everest from Base Camp. The last view of Everest is a few hours back down the trail in Gorak Shep. I stopped on my way and was lucky to get a view amongst all the passing cirrus clouds. When the sky opened up for a brief moment, it was like the seventh veil dropping. The world's tallest mountain has a presence, almost a feeling of divinity.

Compared to that Base Camp is purgatory: rock, jagged pillars of ice, large mountains with steep scree slopes and overhanging precipices of snow that roar down in nightly avalanches. As I hike toward my camp I can see many yaks packed with gear walking amidst a disordered array of yellow, orange, red and green tents scattered across an otherwise grey and white valley. And I can see the Khumbu Glacier, the first treacherous obstacle between Base Camp and the summit. Among all of these things are several pujas, temporary altars built from rock.

Every climbing team will have a puja ceremony at Base Camp before attempting a summit. It is a way for climbers to pay their respects to the gods and goddess spirit of the mountain, asking permission to step on her, basically. The Sherpas believe one should not even sleep on the mountain before undertaking a puja ceremony. It has to be held only on auspicious days and the lama in Pangboche decides what that day will be.

Eventually we find the location where our camp is to be set up, and Andrew, Childon and Miloh set about levelling off areas for our personal sleeping tents with pickaxes and shovels. I grab the camera and film the ice picks hammering the glacial ice. It takes a few hours to level off flat surfaces for all the tents. After achieving a flat square of ice, they place a layer of broken rock and moraine on top, then a tarp, and finally the tent. The rocks on the ice will create a flat base that won't melt as fast as the exposed ice surrounding the tents. As my frozen and rocky sleeping surface is being prepared, I flash back to the night before my departure from Vancouver and my last-minute decision to eject my deluxe Thermarest from one of our bags to make room for more camera equipment. I assured myself in that hasty moment that Asian Trekking would have a Thermarest I could use. And they do, but as I eye the quarter-inch-thick piece of foam that looks like it's been around since the 1980s I lament my decision. Andrew, meanwhile, puts air into his deluxe six-inch-thick Thermarest and pulls out his pillow.

We have a large mess tent that was set up hours before we arrived and waiting inside are the bags we sent ahead in Lukla. I find the large duffel bag with all the food in it and like a savage rip open and barely bother to chew two fruit bars and some beef jerky before swallowing. The mess tent will serve as our dining room and office, where I will spend hours every day transferring footage. A cooking tent and a bathroom tent will go up tomorrow, as well as a shower tent. Don't be fooled: the shower tent and the bathroom tent both look like porta-potties made of soft plastic walls. The shower tent will be empty. To shower means to go into the tent with a bowl of water. To go to the bathroom means to squat over a big blue bucket perched on an edge. The bucket sits in a platform surrounded by rocks on three sides, allowing access to remove it when it is full. Rocks are also piled around each tent to give support as the ground around us melts over the warm season. I am told that in forty days my tent, which is now flush with the surface, will be six feet above our pathways because the ice around us will melt much faster than the ice under our tents. A lot of rock will be moved and sculpted over the course of the season.

There are lots of young men carrying rocks in wicker baskets. In addition to the bathrooms and the tent pads, every year all the stone altars and the work surfaces in kitchen tents must be constructed. All this rockwork happens here every April; by fall, weather and the glacier will sweep it all away as if it's nothing more than a heavy-duty sandcastle.

The yaks and dzokyos have dropped off our loads and are returning to lower altitudes to graze. We won't need pack animals for another forty days. Nothing grows up here; only the moraine expands as the glacier recedes.

As I watch the bustle and hustle and stare at the hundreds of tents everywhere I am blown away by the knowledge that everything has been carried in on the back of a porter or a yak. Dawa Sherpa told me in Kathmandu that for an average expedition on Everest, all the equipment, tents and food can add up to twenty to twenty-five tonnes. One porter carries 30 kilos, so you are talking about thousands of porters carrying loads up to Base Camp. And once all the stuff arrives on this moving and rugged glacier, the camps have to be set up. And this is all just part one. After Base Camp is established the Sherpas start setting up the four successively higher camps up the mountain. It's all rather staggering. Suddenly building pyramids by hand doesn't seem so improbable.

DAY 2: APRIL 21

I wake up to my first morning at Base Camp after a restless night. I experienced a kind of sleep apnea called "periodic breathing." Every time I dozed off I would stop breathing for up to ten seconds and wake up gasping for breath and having an anxiety attack. This is a common side effect of high-altitude, and it is something I will live with for forty days. Dreams are strange, sleep feels shallow, and I experience moments when I'm not sure if I am sleeping or awake. The night is filled with loud crashing sounds—avalanches on Everest and Lhotse. As my tent is perched on the edge of the Khumbu Glacier, I brace myself for the sound of ice rolling my way. But then I realize that if it does come my way, by the time I could get out of my sleeping bag and liner, I would be buried in snow.

Opening the fly on my tent I see Miloh and his assistant assembling a huge parabolic solar cooker between the mess tent and my tent. The cooker is basically an inverted metal umbrella that focuses the sun's rays on a pot of water. It looks like something NASA would set up on a space station and apparently can boil 10 litres of water every thirty-five minutes.

The first priority for Andrew and me this morning is to get solar panels and the rented 1000-watt generator going so we can transfer footage onto hard drives. The nightmare of HD shot on P2 cards is that it must be transferred to two hard drives, a working drive and a backup. It turns out the generator doesn't work well with hard drives: the energy isn't constant and it's not grounded. When I plug in a hard drive a very scary box with an unhappy face pops up saying "Disk is unreadable."

For an hour I believe we have lost everything we have shot to this point. But plugging hard drives into solar panels solves the problem. So the generator will be used for camera batteries and the laptop, and the solar for hard drives. One problem solved, but my anxiety level is still high as I have barely started. I need to find more characters. Making this film is my summit, my money and two months of my life. Failure terrifies me.

DAY 3: APRIL 22

After another wicked night of headaches and popping midnight Advil, I get up thinking I might have to hike down this morning. In the dining tent, Childon tells me the headache and the lack of sleep are normal acclimatization symptoms, but warns me that vomiting would be a bad sign. Childon and Bashista give me some stronger painkillers and tell me to take two pills three times a day.

"Here's to your health and mine," I say, swallowing my first two very large red pills.

"You must drink a lot of water and tea. The air is very dry," cautions Childon. "In the morning, it is very cold and windy, and in the afternoon it can be a hot sun."

This is one of the psychological tensions of being at Base Camp. How do you know if you are suffering from HAPE or HACE, or just AMS, when it all starts with a headache? It is hard to know if it is a normal reaction to the altitude or something more serious because all the symptoms are the same. Bashista says it is very important during the day not to stay inside the tent. There is even less oxygen inside tents than in the thin air outside. I have some swelling around my eyes, but the pills take the edge off. Within an hour we are setting up the camera in front of the Khumbu icefield.

My idea is to shoot a cinéma-vérité documentary. It's a style of filmmaking that started in France in the 1950s, but picked up steam in the US with indie filmmakers like D.A. Pennebaker, the Maysles brothers and Richard Leacock. As D.A. Pennebaker says, "Like a cat who sits in a window, I don't care what happens, I just watch." And that is exactly what I intend Andrew and me to do. Coming from a strong background in fiction filmmaking, this is challenging for Andrew. He wants a shot list; he wants to work as a team. With only two of us here I need us to be able to work apart, both shooting cameras. I need him to trust his intuition and find the shot, not just work off the shot list. He would prefer if I directed and he did all the filming. So we have a few bumps as we begin and I hope I haven't made the wrong choice. I know Andrew has a great eye, and I believe in his talent. I'm just not sure if he trusts my process and style of filmmaking. For the first few days, I decide, we will work together.

Under windy but clear skies, after a few hours of filming climbers coming down the Khumbu Glacier we find our next character, a Nepalese hero and a regular at Everest Base Camp, Apa Sherpa. A small-framed man, Apa is the lead Sherpa for Asian Trekking's eight paying clients. He was born in the village of Thame, which is a two-day walk from here and sits at an elevation of 3,750 metres. Apa has nineteen Everest summits under his belt, the world record. He is going for number twenty this year.

"I have been through the icefield so many times," Apa says, pointing to the glacier behind him. "I first summited in 1990 with the son of Edmund Hillary, Peter Hillary, and Rob Hall. And since 1990 I have summited every year except in 1996. In 1996 I was supposed to join Rob Hall—he asked me many times to join his expedition—but my wife says 'Don't go. We need to build a house in Thame.' So I didn't go that year."

That was the year New Zealand mountaineer and guide Rob Hall died when his group was nailed by a blizzard while making a summit attempt. A total of twelve climbers died on Everest that season. The disaster was immortalized in Jon Krakauer's book *Into Thin Air*.

"You are a smart man, Apa. You listened to your wife," I comment, and we both laugh. But it really is not that funny. More Sherpas have died on the mountain than all the Himalayan climbers from all nations combined.

"This year I am going to go for summit number twenty. I hope I get to number twenty."

As Apa talks, climbers continue to weave slowly down the Khumbu Icefall behind him. None of these people have been to the summit. They are doing what are called rotations. To climb Everest, climbers have to slowly acclimatize their bodies to the high-altitude. Usually there are three rotations as weather permits over a few weeks before they attempt the summit. With his upbringing at 3,750 metres, Apa's physiology is well suited to high-altitudes, so his acclimatization process is different from a Westerner's.

"Tomorrow I go to Camp Two directly, touch Camp Two, come back here. Normally for Western people they go to Camp One and Two. But I don't. I just go straight to Camp Two, then come back here. Then next time I go back to Camp Two, sleep one night, and come back here. And that's it. That's my last acclimatization. Then I go for the summit."

I ask how Everest has changed over the past twenty years since Apa's first summit.

"In 1990 when I summited there was more ice, more snow. Big change now, all rock, and it is very dangerous for climbing." Apa points to ridges of exposed rock that in 1990 were covered by part of the glacier. "We call Everest Chomolungma, mother goddess of the earth. We have to respect her. We should not climb before we do a puja ceremony here first. We have to make Chomolungma happy for a safe climb and [to safely] come back. All the teams participate in pujas. So now they understand. Nobody can go without a ceremony now."

I respect the animist beliefs of the Sherpas. The idea that a mountain or a river can be a god or a goddess makes sense when you look at Chomolungma. The peak is like a breast; the melting water that goes into the valley to nourish people and the crops in the field is the milk that feeds them all.

This year a thirteen-year-old is climbing Everest from the other side. His name is Jordan Romero and his attempt is sparking a lot of debate. He is climbing from the Tibetan side as Nepal won't issue a climbing licence to anyone under sixteen. I ask Apa if he thinks that is too young. He is reluctant to pass judgment, saying only that Everest is hard and requires experience, which he says matters more than age. Good point, given the number of fifty-year-olds here going for their first mountain climb.

As we wrap up with Apa, Meagan comes down from the mountain. She had intended to go to Camp Three, but got sick at Camp Two and had no Tylenol with her so she came down. She also wanted her own satellite phone for communication with Base Camp. She got separated from her Sherpa guide and had no radio. Remembering how a radio had saved her life in the crevasse in Antarctica, she kindly tells her radio guy, Marshall, that she would like to have her own radio for the next rotation on her attempt to climb Lhotse.

A few hours later we meet up with Meagan again at our mess tent. I want to film her and ask for an introduction to Marshall, who is based in their communications tent. I am hoping he will be a character in the documentary.

MEAGAN'S STORY

After tea we go outside and Andrew finds a good spot for the interview on some flat snow framed by ice and rock. Meagan tells me her interest in climbing goes back to when she was a little girl growing up in rural Ontario, where there were hills to climb and bush and trees and swamps to explore. She was a tomboy like me, but while she was climbing ridges, I was riding my banana-seat bike through forest trails and catching frogs and salamanders. Meagan loves mountaineering. That's why she is in the Canadian military. For all the cultural differences, everyone here at Base Camp shares the same passions for adventure and physical challenge. Like lemmings, all of us drawn to the cliff's edge.

Meagan is attempting to summit Lhotse, the peak next to Everest and the fourth-highest mountain in the world. It is connected to Everest by the South Col. To get to the Lhotse summit she will climb the same route up to Everest as far as Camp Three; then she will turn right instead of left to Lhotse's peak. When I ask about her first rotation, Meagan shakes her head. "It went fine up to Camp One. However, I forgot my meds at Base Camp, unfortunately. Beginner's mistake. I went up to Camp Two the next day and I felt fine. However, the headache came back again, and this time I was puking everything I was eating. So I made the decision to come down the following day when it was cold enough and safe enough to come down the Icefall once again."

As she talks I start to feel better about my own high-altitude adjustment misery—the headaches, the nausea, all normal here.

As mentioned, I didn't meet Meagan till we had supper in Kathmandu a few weeks earlier, but I had written about her in the article about my first trek here in 2007. I know she saved a woman's life on her way back down from the summit, so I ask what happened that day. Her story is so compelling and to my knowledge has never really been properly told, so rather than summarize it I am including the full transcript here.

"It was 8,400 metres, just below the balcony. There are two ropes at that steeper section, and I was just behind my Sherpa, Ang Rita. We had stopped and he was preparing the ropes to drop down. I tapped on Ang's shoulder and said, 'Does that climber look okay to you?' Something didn't seem right. He never said anything. He just zoomed down to the next anchor point. So when it was my turn I stopped beside the climber and said, 'Hey, how's it going?' And she—although I didn't know it was a she at that time—mumbled incoherently.

"As she did that I was noticing some things. I noticed her mitts were on the wrong hands, her oxygen mask was not on properly, and she was trying to ask for her goggles. I said 'You don't need your goggles. You need to go down.' Aside from these things that were wrong with her, the time of day was totally wrong. She should be going down. Nobody should be going up at that time of day. She just hadn't made enough progress to be successful in enough time, and the worst part was her carabiner wasn't closed. The carabiner has strength when it is closed, not when it is not. Had she fallen it would not have supported her. So I tried to convince her to come back down, and I'm saying all kinds of things like, 'Come back tomorrow, you'll do it better—whatever, fuck, just come back down, right?'

"And she kinda came on board, so I tried to fix her carabiner and it was really tight and I couldn't loosen it to draw it back and do it properly. Hindsight is 20/20. I should just have used one of mine. And then, by this time, these two other guys were coming down the mountain on my rope. There are only two ropes at this point. And I said, 'Hey, do you guys mind giving me a hand?' So now we are trying to get her down and she falls over, and it is very steep. She is lying face into the mountain and she is not even moving under her own power at all. So now we were really trying to place her feet. We weren't doing it right and I remember stopping at one point and thinking, 'Oh my god, we are not doing this right. We are not getting her air fast enough and we are not moving her down the mountain fast enough.' The first rule of climbing rescue is get them more oxygen and then get them down fucking fast. And we weren't doing either very well. And I remember going, 'Okay, Sherpa guy, have you ever done this before, have you learned this anywhere?' and he's like, 'No.' Great. I ask, 'Chuck, have you ever been involved in a situation like this?' 'No.'

"And I have never done this before either so we all just have to go by the seat of our pants. I'm saying, 'Okay, we know that she needs oxygen, so let's get her oxygen. I have some oxygen.' I even had an extra tank in my bag, so I thought okay, we will use that. We kind of moved her down a little ways but it was really messed up. So then I said, 'How about you guys go down and get some help, like maybe send somebody up, whatever, do what you need to do.'

"I look in my bag and I'm like, fuck, I thought I had another oxygen tank, but I didn't. I only had the one I was using. But I felt fine so I put my oxygen mask on her. One of the other things we noticed was not only was her oxygen mask off her face, in a way it was suffocating her, blocking the air from going into her. Her oxygen line was wrapped around her neck. This goes from bad to worse.

"Weight matters very much in climbing. When my Sherpa and I first decided to go up that day, I figured we would always be together, so we were only going to bring the one knife between the two of us, and he had the knife, so I couldn't cut the oxygen line around her neck. Then I'm trying to unwrap it and trying not to wrap it tighter because I couldn't figure out which way to go. So she has oxygen now. I open my suit, trying to give her some body heat.

"I'm all alone with her at this point, telling her some awful jokes. Then her breathing starts getting really weird, very not good, and she is starting to pass out for longer stretches of time. I estimate I was there for forty minutes.

"It occurs to me that help is going to take longer coming from below than it is from above. Then I notice two climbers coming down so I kneel down beside her so they know something is wrong. It is a Western climber and a Sherpa, and the Western climber leans across to me and asks, 'Is there a problem?' He said it with such authority I thought, this guy is a guide, so I tell him everything that has happened. And then he says, 'My name is Dave Hahn and I'm a guide.' And I'm like, 'I know who you are,' because he has a reputation for the most rescues. He tells me to get my oxygen back on and he starts swearing, 'She's not going to fuckin' die, and we are not going to fuckin' die trying to save her, but she *might* fuckin' die.' And I have been sitting here watching this girl die.

"She had HACE, and I had dexamethasone, but only in pill form, which is not very good when you are unconscious. So I crush the pills and put it under her tongue, hoping maybe some of it will get into her system with a bit of water. Dave Hahn takes over at this point. He has the vial form of dexamethasone so he asks his Sherpa for the first aid kit and gets the vial. Then he's warming up the vial between his hands and asks the Sherpa to hand him the needle, and as he does I can see the needle go ping down the mountain.

"Now I'm like, 'For fuck's sake, this is getting worse.' And he's like, 'Tell me there is another needle in that box.' And the Sherpa rummages around for what seems like a second too long, then pulls out a big gauge needle with a syringe, and just like *Pulp Fiction*, Dave shoves the needle right into her thigh, and she doesn't even flinch. I'm like, 'Wow, she's really going to die. This is interesting. I have never been in this situation.' And then they started bringing her down. I had a Prusik, which is a sling, so she could be lowered down. I was carrying her pack, and now Dave gave her his oxygen. Using the Prusik the Sherpa lowered her down from above while Dave, with no oxygen, is guiding her feet. They do it for a while, and then Dave of course gets out of breath because he has no oxygen. Eventually they recruit more people, and Dave backs off and more people are involved but Dave is directing. He keeps asking me to leave at this point but I'm saying no. The third time he says, 'Meagan, go down,' I was noticing my breathing was getting short and shallow. 'Fuck,' I thought, 'this isn't good,' so I gave him her pack and I went down to Camp Four. At that point my Sherpa comes out with a cup of tea, and I'm like, 'Hi, Ang.' I wasn't going to apologize for being late."

THE PUJA

The mountain is alive. I wake in the middle of the night to what climbers call the Everest lullaby: a symphony of sounds, popping, cracking, crashing, rushing water and the sound of the wind. Mix that with my rapid heartbeat and shallow breathing and you have the soundtrack for a Hitchcock film.

Andrew's energy is low today and he is coming down with a cold. I think we are both still struggling with symptoms of AMS. Over breakfast he tells me his compass is acting strangely and that the same whacko magnetic energy could affect our hard drives. The thought that I could lose my footage if something damages my hard drives is so frigging scary—another layer of stress.

Despite that we have a good and productive day filming a puja ceremony. As we approach the altar of rocks and burning juniper, Andrew sets up the camera. I am offered a seat next to a Sherpa who introduces himself to me as the head ice doctor at Base Camp, Ang Nima Sherpa. I take a seat on a Thermarest lying on the ground next to him. As I cross the filmmaker's line, from observer to participant, I try not to be aware of Andrew's lens and where he's directing his attention. I hope he's getting all of it, the semicircle of people sitting around the puja and the fold-out table with drinks, bowls of rice and popcorn, yak butter and plates of food. I also have a camera in hand, a smaller one, so I focus it and put it on my lap and just get close-ups for cutaways for the scene, if we use it. That is the crazy thing about this style of documentary filmmaking: you shoot eighty hours, you use one.

Scattered around the base of the altar are climbing ropes, ice picks, helmets—all the critical gear the climbers want blessed for their expedition. A lama, possibly from Pangboche Monastery, stands next to the altar chanting. Someone gives me a cup of tea. Ang Nima tells me to throw some of the food to the gods for blessings on the mountain and to eat some. We each take turns throwing rice, eating popcorn, shooting back rum and drinking Everest beer. There's something kind and open about the ceremony. It's a sharing ritual, and the Sherpas are keeping the sacred connection to the mountain alive.

After the puja Andrew, Bashista, Childon and I film an interview with Ang Nima at the mess tent for the nine ice doctors Ang has working under him. I am curious about what they do. And I am shocked to find out that before anybody starts climbing this mountain, these guys show up to set up the lines and the ladders. Their job is to go to the most dangerous, most volatile part of the mountain every day. The ice collapses, it moves, it crunches, so their job is to go in to make sure their lines are okay, to make sure the ladders fit properly over the crevasses. The ice doctors are the first to arrive at Base Camp and the last to leave. This year they have put forty-five ladders on the mountain. And every day they will go back up the icefall to check on them. The problem with anchoring a ladder into ice and snow on a glacier is that by day the sun's reflections off the glacier cause things to melt and the metal to expand. By night, as it gets colder, the glacier shifts and moves up to four inches a day. So a safe ladder one day can be a dangerous ladder the next.

Ang says in broken English that this year it took two weeks for the nine guys to fix the ropes and ladders through the Icefall to Camp One. Once they did that, Sherpas from the various expedition companies started going up and setting up Camps One and Two. Again, tents, food and sleeping bags for all the clients had to be carried up.

I appreciate the wisdom Ang Nima has about the ice, much like the Inuit elders I met while filming my first documentary in the High Arctic in 2007. It is a traditional wisdom passed on from one generation to the next, not through a course in a classroom with a textbook. His knowledge is about all the properties of frozen water—not molecules, atoms and periodic tables, but texture, colour and shape. One of the Inuit elders told me it was getting hard now to read the ice in the Arctic because it was melting from the bottom. It wasn't the sun melting the ice from the top; it was the ocean melting the ice from the bottom.

7 P.M.

I tried having a cup of coffee this afternoon but after a few sips my heart was beating like crazy. Both Andrew and I have a resting heartbeat of ninety-six. Every exertion leaves us breathless. It's all part of the challenge of working at high-altitudes. Other challenges come in the night. It gets damp in the tent, and the exterior of my sleeping bag is covered with dew by 8 p.m. It gets so cold in the evenings I just want to go into my sleeping bag with a hot water bottle and snuggle it like a teddy bear. But sleeplessness is a common symptom of AMS, and spending twelve hours in a cold and damp tent when you can't sleep makes for a long night. I long for the first light to come up as it dries the dew and brings the only real sleep I get, between 5 and 7 a.m. That leaves a lot of time for an idle mind and an uncomfortable body.

Why did I leave the comfortable and the known for this gut-wrenching pain and loneliness? What am I fighting for? To prove I can do it? I knew this place had dark shadows before I came, so why was I driven to put myself inside them for forty days?

The entire camp is just an 80-acre parking lot full of tents erected on glacial ice and moraine. By day the melting glacier runoff creates streams that grow larger each day, and at night they all freeze. The ground is constantly shifting. Today I twice stepped on a frozen surface and my feet punched through to cold running water. Fortunately I had dry boots and socks to change into.

Tomorrow I am going to film the radio guy working for Asian Trekking. I suspect if the weather continues to be sunny, summits may start to happen in early May, so I am under pressure to lock in my other characters. I finish the day reading from one of the two books I brought to Base Camp,

The Language of Vision. At the beginning is this quote from Rainer Maria Rilke: "This in the end is the only kind of courage that is required of us: the courage to face the strangest, most unusual, most inexplicable experiences that can meet us."

I hope I have the courage for thirty-five more days at Base Camp.

LOGISTICS

Every expedition has a communications tent and a radio person. Asian Trekking's communication guy is Marshall Thompson, a photographer and blogger from Utah. Marshall spends a lot of time in a green tent that is set up with a satellite radio receiver and Internet so he can file a daily blog. The tent also contains a beige metal box that regulates the generator so people can use their battery rechargers. I could have used one of those myself. But none of this comes cheap. The going rate is $3,500 for 500MB of data. That is more than the average Sherpa makes in a year.

Marshall has a blond beard and moustache and blue eyes, and so far I have only seen him wearing a wool Nepali hat with peace signs on it, army pants and a big black down jacket. Marshall used to be in the American military. He served in Iraq and now wants to study international law. He is married with two kids and lives with his family in Logan, Utah.

Marshall is at Base Camp because a friend of his who knew Apa (who has lived in Utah for the past few years so his kids could go to school there) invited him at the last minute. "My friend called me up and said, 'Hey, we know you do photography, we know you do blogging. Would you like to go to Base Camp and help Apa out?' I said yes. And he said, 'Okay, you have two weeks before you leave.' And that's how I got here. I started growing out my beard immediately."

Marshall grins and strokes his beard. Although he hasn't known Apa long, he already has great respect for him. "The first time I met Apa I was really nervous because here's this hero and I was a bit worried that he would be unexceptional, but he wasn't. He was very exceptional, but in different ways than you would expect. It was his humility and his sense of humour and his kindness that just bowled me over. That's why I was keen to come. I had to quit my job, and I won't see my wife and kids for two months, which is really hard, but it is absolutely worth it to help Apa out in any way. I keep thinking about him in contrast with Tiger Woods. You got two Buddhist athletes, and one, we know full well what he did. He thought that he was best in the world and he started feeling privileged and entitled. And then you have Apa, on the other hand, who I don't think has felt entitled to anything in his life.

"I am a very religious person, and I just love the Sherpas' belief that Mount Everest is a goddess and I am very thankful to spend some time here at the foot of the goddess."

Marshall pauses, and we both smile. I like him immediately. I ask him what his impressions are of the place.

"It is sort of anarchy, but somehow things get done." He chuckles to himself. "One of the first things we did here is I went to one of the meetings where they talked about fixing ropes, and it was bizarre. There literally isn't anybody running the meeting. There is no chairperson or Robert's Rules of Order. It is just a bunch of guys sort of trying to agree, and it is not like these people are very agreeable. They are very nice, but we are talking about some very intense people who know their stuff and there are a lot of leaders among them. And somehow from this there has to be a leader and followers, so it was really interesting to see how it all sussed out. And it happens every year, so God bless them."

After leaving Marshall I run into a young kid with long black hair in his eyes and a big white-toothed smile. It seems we've both heard of each other. Arjun is from India. He lives in Delhi and is sixteen years old. He is hoping to become one of the youngest climbers to ever summit Everest, and the youngest Indian. He tells me he is keen to be in the film. Andrew sets up the camera down a small path of loose rock next to a boulder the size of an SUV. Boulders like this one are scattered all over the camp. Given that the ground is melting and shifting every day, they make me wary, but Arjun looks relaxed standing next to it. I ask him where he got the inspiration to climb.

"In India, I am just a normal kid. I have just entered my twelfth grade. I am an average student, and I play soccer. In India, everyone is running to be a doctor or engineer. Nobody is thinking you could make a career out of this also." He gestures to the Khumbu Icefall. "Many people are behind me, inspiring me. Apa Sherpa has been a real inspiration for me. And I have some really good army people back in my country who inspired me to do this peak. You can be a professional mountaineer, you can see the real heaven, that's out here. The aspects of life that you are not able to see there, you can see here. You can feel the danger, you can feel the risk out here, and you are enjoying your life."

"What's the biggest risk for you on the mountain?" I ask.

Again Arjun turns and faces the glacier. "The biggest risk is the Khumbu Icefall. It's one of the most difficult things you can ever face in your mountaineering career. It keeps moving all the time. And the other big risk is the altitude. After 8,000 metres you don't understand who you are, you are half-dead, you are only supported by a Sherpa, and then you just keep walking."

"Have you had any frightening moments?"

"I have had one frightening moment in the Khumbu Icefall. There was a slow climber in front of us and we could not overtake him and we could just hear the ice cracking around us. We were a bit late, so we were just praying the cracking wouldn't come up to us because you can't run away from there, and it can just come up to you anytime." After a pause he adds, "Destiny also plays a part here. Avalanches will keep coming—it is a part of mountaineering, so you have to be well and face them. I am not worried about avalanches." At that he winks and smiles and walks away.

Oh, the bravado of sixteen! I know that attitude: I had it too until I actually had a few close calls with the shadows of death. Caution comes with humility. I like Arjun. He is comfortable being himself when the camera is on and is well spoken and funny. And he has agreed to take a camera and film a video diary on the mountain as he summits.

I first gravitated to the idea of sending cameras up with my characters before I came here as a way of showing the summits without making them the focus of the film. Also we live at a time when everyone has a camera on their phone so I liked the idea of weaving this modern idea into an old story. As well, the video diary has an intimacy to it I can't get when pointing a camera at people.

The other advantage of course is logistics. I want to follow several characters and with only Andrew and me here to shoot the film it would be impossible to follow more than one character up the mountain. This way we can follow several people and I can indulge my interest in the wide variety of people and motivations, ranging from the nationalistic—people who want to put their country's flag on top of the mountain—to the corporate—a team sponsored by Hanes underwear is weaving the idea of people finding their own Everest into their marketing strategy. And then there are those like Arjun, Meagan and others who are driven by personal desires and have paid an expedition company to take them up.

After talking to Arjun I realize sending cameras is also safer for my characters and for me. Following a sixteen-year-old up Everest might inspire him to take chances in front of the camera he wouldn't take otherwise. In Jon Krakauer's book, one of the questions that gets tossed around is the idea that his presence was a contributing factor to the disaster. He was a journalist writing for *Outside* magazine about two climbing companies and their paid clients. A million people would read that article so, naturally, the companies wanted to get their clients to the top. The world was watching. At the end of the day I don't think Krakauer was to blame. We all have to take personal responsibility for what we do. Still, I am glad sending cameras up with my clients sidetracks the potential for my involvement in a tragedy.

I slip and slide on the scree and ice back to my dining tent for lunch. After, Andrew, Bashista, Childon and I plan to find the Himalayan Rescue Association's medical tent somewhere in the chaos of Base Camp. No paths, no roads or permanent trails anywhere through a constantly shifting physical environment makes finding people nearly impossible without the help of Bashista and Childon. And I chuckle to myself as I look at my film crew and realize together we are a Buddhist, a Hindu, a recovering Catholic and an atheist—all of us hiking around the belly of a mountain revered as a goddess.

THE HIMALAYAN
RESCUE TENT

The Himalayan Rescue Association (HRA) is a voluntary non-profit organization that was created in 1973 to provide medical services in Nepal's Himalayan mountains. They have a permanent office in a Khumbu village called Pheriche, which is a long day's hike from here and sits at an altitude of 4,373 metres. The medical tent at Base Camp was first established in 2003. It gets set up in early April and remains till the end of the climbing season at the end of May. The tent is a white half-dome with a red cross on the front above the door. Inside are two beds, a Persian rug, some tables, a cooler and a radio, and stethoscopes hang from its frame. In charge this year is a forty-something American emergency physician named Dr. Luanne Freer who developed an interest in altitude medicine while working as a doctor at Yellowstone National Park. Luanne tells us she volunteered for the HRA clinic in Pheriche because she really believes in their mandate, which is to charge foreigners for health services but to give services free to the local Sherpa people.

They see just about everything in the HRA tent at Base Camp, she adds. "We see people who suffer from traumatic injuries from a fall. We see people dying in the Icefall when a serac of ice falls at the wrong time. We have never had anyone die in our tent. I would like to say it is because we are such good physicians, but the reality is it is so difficult to get down from high on the mountain, people often die on the way down."

I am relieved to know nobody has died in the tent, as this is where I will crawl if my AMS develops into something more serious. No dialing 911 up here, I'm thinking, as the doctor continues to show me around.

She tells me about her work developing a technical rescue team run by Sherpas who would be able to deal more effectively with some problems on the mountain. "I think the case I will never forget was in 2003 when a twenty-three-year-old Sherpa died from appendicitis. Everybody in the developed world knows that is a relatively easy problem to treat, but when it takes four days to get someone down from a high camp we don't have a chance to get them to surgery. And to watch someone die from something we can treat is tragic, frustrating, and we need to make things better."

"When there is a problem on this mountain, is there radio contact with this tent? How do you participate in this process when something starts to go wrong up there?" I ask.

"When there is a problem, we keep our radios open. We have a radio system that allows us to have contact with the teams on the mountain and that is very valuable. We have folks up there who have medication but they are not quite sure how to use it so we get involved in that decision. If there is someone who collapses high in the death zone above 8,200 metres we can help find resources from down here, get the teams together, find out where there is oxygen and Sherpas who can help, to coordinate a joint rescue."

This sounds reassuring, but even the best rescue plans don't always work. Everest is known for the many deaths on the mountain, including disturbing stories like the one of British climber David Sharp who died above Camp Four in 2006 while on a solo ascent of the mountain. Over forty climbers are said to have passed him without offering assistance en route to their own summit attempt. Sharp was one of four Asian Trekking clients that died on Everest in 2006. His body still sits there next to another climber who died in 1996. Everyone calls this climber Green Boots. He sits about three hundred metres beyond Camp Four next to the trail, a macabre reminder that not all dreams and aspirations end well.

For those who are rescued, the clinic is well stocked with equipment that can handle the altitude. Much of it is solar powered. There's a heart monitor that measures blood pressure, heart rhythm and the level of oxygen in a patient's body, along with several medications and the usual medical supplies you'd see in most clinics. But what most clinics don't have (and don't need) is a remarkable piece of equipment called a hyperbaric chamber.

Luanne walks over to a red canvas backpack and dumps out what looks like a big red duffel bag. She explains that they can put a person inside it, then pump up the pressure, taking people from 5,300 to 3,300 metres in a matter of minutes. "That quick descent, although it is artificial and temporary, can be life saving. We have had patients in this bag cyclically for eight to ten hours. So when they are in, they feel good, their headache gets better, they are breathing better. Then they have to get out for a drink, and I have had them look at me and say 'get me back in there.'"

Luanne offers to demonstrate the bag on one of us. Andrew is filming, so I am the guinea pig. And I am thrilled. My brain is doing a happy dance with the idea of more oxygen, even for just a minute. I take off my hiking boots and slide into the red canvas duffel bag, Luanne gives me her altimeter watch and zips me in. There is a clear plastic window where my face is so they can communicate with me. They clip the blood oxygen machine to my finger to get a reading.

"You are going in with a blood oxygen [level] of 75 and a heart rate of 101 at an altitude of 17,477 feet [5,327 metres]," Luanne tells me, adding that if I walked into an emergency room in Vancouver with that blood oxygen level they would put me in intensive care. But here, it's normal. Like I keep saying, Base Camp is a strange place.

She zips the bag closed and starts pumping oxygen into it with a foot pump. Within a minute the headache that has had my brain in a grip for days loosens up. My breathing feels better. My blood oxygen goes up to 79 and my heart rate down to 82. Already down to 3,650 metres. My oxygen saturation peaks at 86 percent. The watch shows me at 3,353 metres.

I love this bag. I want this bag. And then Luanne tells me they are bringing me back to Base Camp. Like a child safe and warm in a womb I want to yell no, leave me in here, I don't want to come out. But I don't, and within seconds I'm back to 5,327 metres. Reality bites. As I extricate myself from the bag I ask Luanne if they perform coroner services in the event of a death on the mountain. She pauses a moment before answering. "It's a really interesting question in Nepal. We have so many different cultures, religions, represented here in Base Camp. And for every different language spoken here there is probably a different view of death and how a person would want their body handled. Many expeditions, before their clients even leave their country of origin, have to check a box on their permit application to indicate what they want done with their body if they die on Everest. Do you want it left where you die, do you want it to be brought down, do you want it flown back to your country, or do you want to be cremated? At first I thought it was an odd question but it is kind of a nice reality check for people who feel the safety of being guided perhaps to realize there is a real risk here."

If Andrew or I die we are signed up for the only affordable option, cremation at the Everest graveyard. It dawns on me that with no police, no coroner and no investigation into cause of death, Everest would be a good place to commit murder—a bit like the Wild West, though once people reach Camp Four it's oxygen, not gold, that people will commit crimes for.

Luanne brings me back to earth, telling me the most common problem they see at Base Camp is the high-altitude cough, which they call the "Khumbu cough."

"Currently there is a lot of debate about what causes this cough, but all of us agree there is some component of the really dry cold air here that causes the bronchial tree to crack and go into spasm and cause this horrible cough. It is not a cough we can treat with antibiotics or any of the typical treatments from home. We use a lot of prevention strategies but that's it; for eight years running now it is the most common complaint, and is also one of the main reasons people have to leave an expedition, because the cough is that bad. It can cause ribs to fracture. That's our dirge at Base Camp."

I know what she means by "dirge." I hear it every night, a sad chorus of coughing, in stark contrast to the relative silence of my country home on 8 acres where all I hear is the occasional sound of croaking frogs. Breathing cold, dry, oxygen-deprived air makes my throat thirst for the lush moisture of the rainforest.

In the afternoon, it starts to snow. I feel chilled, so I retreat to my sleeping bag with two hot water bottles. When living in a tent at high-altitude for forty days, getting a chill is not a great situation. My fingers are numb despite wearing two pairs of gloves. My handwriting looks like a five-year-old's. I put one hot water bottle by my feet, one by my belly. I give up trying to write full sentences and then I give up writing. I have a book but after a few minutes of trying to focus and read I put that down too. I think these are mild symptoms of hypoxia, the clinical term for re-duced oxygen to the brain. Compared to other cells, brain cells are really sensitive to hypoxia and they quickly begin to die without oxygen—not a comforting thought, so I occupy myself by counting thread weaves on tent panels.

It's bloody cold and the inside of my tent is full of ice crystals, but tonight I will leave the tent vents open. It goes against the idea of trying to get the tent warm but in this thin atmosphere I need fresh air coming in. Childon told me those candle lanterns are not a good idea at high-altitude. Flames burn oxygen. So burning candles in my tent was starving me of oxygen. Probably why my headaches are so bad. There is no getting warm in this place. Not even from the small flame of a candle.

EQUIPMENT

❧

Once again my day begins with a headache and I pop another 400 mg painkiller and drag myself out of the tent. This morning I will interview Meagan as she preps for her next rotation up to Camp Three. I want to shoot some footage of all the gear a climber carries up the mountain with them. And then I am meeting the Sirdar who works for Asian Trekking. He is too shy to be filmed but is open to a cup of tea.

Meagan's tent is just up a small ridge from mine, one of six yellow tents in a row right at the base of the Khumbu Glacier. Inside her two-man tent, Meagan is inspecting her equipment for any damage that might need repair before her next rotation. On her Thermarest are an ice pick, a harness and crampons.

She carries trekking poles and an ice axe with its handle wrapped in foam and duct tape because even through gloves, the handle can feel really cold. She has crampons to go onto the bottom of her climbing boots. They have spikes to grip the snow and a plastic plate that helps prevent snow from balling up under the soles. And then there's the harness. Meagan picks it up to show it to me.

"The harness is actually a pretty heavy piece of equipment," Meagan says. It looks like an elaborate tool belt. She shows me various things that are hanging off it, including a tool for rappelling called an ATC device and some red and black cords called Prusiks that she can use if she falls into a crevasse. In essence, they are loops that she can attach to the rope and put her feet and hands in to climb up and out. Meagan also shows me the knife she carries. Then she pulls out what looks like a small aluminum bag, which she calls a rest stop bag.

"I have been on mountains where you can't step anywhere without stepping in people's crap. It is pretty gross," she says. "What we do here is part of Asian Trekking's Eco Everest. The bag is made of a tin foil type of material. Inside it has toilet paper with antiseptic wipe, and another grey bag you pull out and into which you do your deed. There is a powder in the bag that turns the contents into a gel form really quickly, and it's not stinky. It's a handy thing to have for human waste that you don't want to leave on the mountain or have it flow into a water system."

Eco Everest was Dawa's idea, which he introduced in 2007 after he saw all the garbage at Base Camp. He started a cleanup project, demonstrated the use of solar parabolic cookers to boil water and introduced the toilet bags for his climbers and Sherpas to use. It is a small dent with still hundreds of other climbers not using them, but a positive step just the same. I ask Meagan if she is nervous the bags will break in her knapsack but she assures me the tin foil material doesn't rip. I think there's something poetic about the idea of people carrying their shit around.

For clothes, she packs from the bottom up, starting with liner socks, wool socks, and boots; then women's boxers, merino wool long johns and Gore-Tex pants with a full side zip for breathing room. On top she packs a sports bra, wool t-shirt, long-sleeved sweatshirt and a heavy fleece and Gore-Tex jacket for when the sun goes down. Meagan also has a down jacket in her pack to put on when she takes breaks—added benefit: it makes a good pillow.

As well as clothes, Meagan carries a medications bag with Tylenol, Diamox (for acclimatizing) and dexamethasone pills (and the injectable form) for cerebral edema. She also carries a stronger painkiller in case of a bad fall, Gravol for nausea, and a steroid inhaler in case she has difficulty breathing.

"Congestion happens a lot at high-altitude," Meagan explains, "because the cold dry air dries out all the linings in your nasal passage and the body produces excess mucus."

Yup, this is what these people call a good time. Me too, as I am willing to suffer for it. After a thank you and a high five, I leave Meagan to finish her packing and mental preparation and go look for the Sirdar who works for Asian Trekking to find out just how much gear has to be carried up the mountain with the climbers. Most of the climbers on paid expeditions carry nothing but a daypack up the mountain. The Sirdar is the lead Sherpa who makes sure everything their clients will need is waiting for them as they ascend to the higher camps. This entails coordinating the transport of all the clients' luggage from Kathmandu to Lukla and from Lukla to Base Camp, and then organizing the logistics of setting up the four camps up the mountain.

I calculate that with nine paying clients, a relatively small group compared to some companies here, the Sirdar for Asian Trekking will have to send up sixty-three bottles of oxygen. That's at least thirty trips up the mountain just to drop off oxygen at the camps. Most of it has to go to Camp Three and Camp Four. And of course the tents, stoves, food and sleeping bags for four camps—mind-boggling.

On the subject of oxygen bottles, there are two types of oxygen tanks I have seen in tents around Base Camp: big ones and small, thinner ones. The small ones weigh 3.5 kg (6 pounds) and hold 1,240 litres of oxygen, and the larger ones weigh 7 kg and hold 1,800 litres. The smaller ones are made in Russia, the larger ones in the USA. The main advantage of the smaller bottles is weight. You can carry two instead of one and get 40 percent more oxygen. You can also have a backup should one fail. And they do fail. Valves get frozen, regulators break, and cold temperatures can reduce the volume of oxygen in a tank by as much as 25 percent.

The advantage of the bigger bottles is that fewer people use them so there's less chance of having one stolen.

DAY 7: APRIL 26

We've completed our first week at Base Camp and I haven't had a shower since Namche. Maybe when the weather warms up. In the meantime I make do with a small wash with a morning bowl of hot water boiled by Miloh and delivered to my tent by his assistant. Andrew and I get this luxury every morning.

I decide the cure for Western entitlement is just to pull the plug. Deprivation teaches appreciation for small things.

After downloading footage in the morning, I spend the afternoon filming Meagan, Marshall and Arjun. With signed release forms in hand, I now have some great characters for the film and I'm getting excited.

Meagan leaves tomorrow at 4 a.m. for a rotation up to Camp Three, the final rotation before her summit push. I am sending a small video camera with her to film some video diary of herself on the mountain. We will film her early morning departure.

I hear that the wind is blowing at 80 kilometres per hour on the summit, typical for this time of year, apparently. "Winds can be the killer up there for sure," Meagan says. "Winds are cold, winds can bring precipitation, winds are freezing, and if they are strong enough they can blow you off the mountain, literally. So wind is something as climbers we take under serious consideration—as well as temperature, of course. That's the other factor in the game here—you don't want to be freezing up on the mountain."

Before coming here I didn't understand why everyone goes up for a summit push at the same time. The climbing season is two months long. But I get it now. The peak usually has a strong wind blowing on it every day except for a few days in the spring. And everyone here is waiting for one of those few days. That is the weather window: blue skies, no wind. At 8,850 metres, the peak of Everest sits at the same altitude most commercial airliners fly at and is home to the jet stream. The monsoon season usually begins at the end of May and just before it hits there is usually a window, a calm before the storm moment. And that's when the climbing frenzy begins. After weeks of practice runs mixed with a lot of idle time they all run at once.

I share my puja story with Meagan and remark on having seen her walking around one, apparently engaged in some sort of prayer. Smiling, she replies, "Anytime I go into the mountains in the Himalaya here, before I go up and after I come down, I circle the puja altar, which the Sherpas use to pay respect to the goddess—in this case, of Mt. Everest.

"I am not Buddhist, I am not Sherpa, but why not take the time to pay respect to the mountain and the challenge that lies ahead? It is a good time also to focus and to bring yourself into focusing on what you are going to do because you don't want to have your mind all scattered. That's why circling the puja is something I do. The Sherpa probably think I am crazy because it probably has nothing to do with what they do. But again, everyone has their own ritual, like a baseball player who wears the same socks for the whole series, you know. This is just something I do. When I come down, I circle it just to close off the cycle and complete it and say thank you for a successful expedition."

I get it. I left the Catholic Church as a rebellious teenager but I have a medal of a saint pinned to my bra above my heart. And when the shit hits the fan in my life I usually crank out a few Hail Marys.

Meagan and I talk about the ladders she'll have to climb—fifty-two of them on the mountain this year, some leaning the way they would on the side of a house, others completely horizontal. These are the difficult ones, she says. Even though there are ropes on either side to hang onto, they're fairly slack. "You have to lean forward to create some tension on the ropes, and that can be tricky when you have to look down," she explains. "Some of the crevasses where there are ladders may not seem deep because there is a lot of snow under them, so they are pretty easy to go over. But some of them are deep, dark and blue, and you can't see the bottom, and if you are going over by yourself, it is kind of sketchy. You are clipped in for safety in the event that you fall, but it's all a perception game."

What I like about Meagan is that she's willing to admit to being scared—it makes what she does all the more relatable. She tells me a story about a Sherpa who nearly fell off a ladder into a deep crevasse just a few days earlier. As it happened, she was holding the rope for him on one side of the ladder and nearly got pulled into the crevasse herself. "He was dangling, hanging off the ladder, and all the Sherpas immediately reacted. I got out of the way—I was majorly out of breath because I'd had quite a scare. Of course not as much as this particular Sherpa, who was dangling there. He was so calm, cool and collected—again, his mates there were helping him out, they pulled him out, and by the time I caught my breath, he had crossed and had a big smile on his face like, 'Whoo!'

"It just goes to show how much these guys do to get Western climbers up the mountain. They really risk their lives and it is awesome they are willing to do it. I'm pretty grateful."

I can see Meagan's hands are getting cold so we wrap up the interview. I ask her who she is closest to in her life, and she says her family. Her mom doesn't like her passion for climbing. In fact, she says with a smile, her whole family isn't really into it, but they understand it is something she wants to do, and therefore they are very supportive. "My mom sent some letters I can read along the way, and my sister gave me a letter that says, 'Open this when you're having a really bad day.'" Meagan smiles again. "I haven't had to open it yet."

THE CANADIANS

Our day begins at 3:45 a.m. to film Meagan's departure for her rotation up to Camp Three. Andrew is still fighting a cold and I am still suffering from headaches. The wind blows and another avalanche echoes. Knowing people are on the mountain makes the rumbles more frightening. Apa is also up already and lighting the puja at the base of the Khumbu Glacier. I can smell burning juniper as Andrew and I scramble in the cold and dark. It is still pitch black. Meagan walks around the small tower of stones three times and her Sherpa guide stands before it, saying a quiet prayer and throwing some rice.

It seems crazy to go through an ice maze filled with crevasses in the dark, but in fact her decision to do so is a mark of her experience. The Khumbu Icefall is unstable when the sun hits in daylight. Getting a few hours up in the dark while the ice is more stable is a smart thing to do. Still I worry as Andrew, Apa, Marshall and I watch the small light of her headlamp disappear into the dark.

When I came here I thought I would make a film about how fucked up this all is, how crazy that the world's highest mountain has been commercialized. But the humility forced by my own physical challenges, along with the emotional and mental strain, has put my own ego back in a box. Rather than judging the people I'm meeting I am now inspired by them and feel honoured that they have opened their lives to me.

There is more spiritual energy here than in most cathedrals. I feel the spirit of Chomolungma. I look up and see the changing light, the fast winds; I hear the cracks and groans of the glacier opening herself to feed the lower fields, putting drinking water in our mouths. I think of the pujas, the burning juniper and the prayers—not of praise for some omnipotent god, but of respect for a mountain. I had planned to say how odd it is that people talk of the spirituality of the place, given all the human excrement, garbage and dead bodies on the mountain. I mean, how can something sacred be so abused at the same time? Now I realize that is the paradox of being human. We sing church hymns saying God is love, then we go to war. We are messy contradictions.

Apa is also leaving on a rotation today, taking a group up to Camp Two. Dressed in a big red down jacket and shades, he looks like a very styling Sherpa. He returns to the kitchen tent to organize the other clients for today's climb. They are all a little slower to get up and get organized. While we wait for them, Apa explains that after the rotations he will judge whether all the climbers are fit enough for the summit push. He and his climbing Sherpas decide who they think is going to make it, and who they think will not. "If they don't feel good, we don't want to push it. You know Everest is always there. They can try next time. Life is more important than Everest."

Apa explains how the climbers and Sherpas are paired. "Meagan is climbing Lhotse, so she is climbing with Pemba Sherpa because he has climbed Lhotse many times. All the climbers have their own climbing Sherpa, so they will take care of them. I just give them advice and oversee everything. There is a lot of pressure, you know, not easy, we have to take care of many things." I can see Apa's stress. His smile is strained. Being responsible for people's lives weighs heavily on him. Asian Trekking has lost clients. All these expedition companies probably have.

I have heard two different weather reports for the next few days. One suggests sun and little wind, and one calls for snow. I ask Apa what he has heard. "There are too many weather reports here," he says with a laugh, "but we check out many different reports for weeks to see which one is the most accurate, then we go from there. Everest is hard and can be windy all the time, but we are looking for less wind."

It's true: everybody here has their own weather reports and some are quite guarded about them. For all the science and technology, weather prediction is still guesswork. And it is one thing to watch the news to find out whether you need to bring an umbrella on your trip to the store tomorrow, but a mistaken weather report here can have much more dire consequences.

After interviewing Apa and filming Arjun and a few other clients as they head off on their second rotation, we return to our kitchen tent for a late breakfast of potato pancakes, which along with pappadums is my favourite meal here at Base Camp. Miloh is happy because for the first time I ask for seconds.

Hours later I check in with Marshall at the communication tent about how Meagan's climb up the Icefall went. She left six hours ago so she should be at Camp Two by now. I find him there alone in his big parka, looking at weather maps on his laptop. "Meagan is doing really great," he says. "She called on the radio around nine this morning saying that she had reached Camp One. And we set our next radio communication for 6 p.m. today."

I drink a cup of tea with Marshall as he tells me about his plans to go to law school in the fall to study international human rights, something he feels very strongly about. "I have seen a lot of violations so I want to do something about it. I am an Iraq war veteran, and it was really hard to be involved in some of the things I was involved in, so I want to do something to make it better."

"It must be hard to be both a spiritual person and a soldier."

"It is hard," he says. "I think the wounds cut deeper that way, but it's the way I am." He looks out the tent's plastic window at the view over the glacier. After a few moments of silence I ask him what he is writing in his blog today. His warm smile returns as he says, "the Bad Finns."

I know exactly who he's talking about. There are a few Finnish groups at Base Camp this year. The two climbing with Asian Trekking, we call the Good Finns. The three camped across from Andrew and me—hard-drinking, loud, cigar-smoking, stay-up-late-talking-about-women guys—are the Bad Finns. Marshall reads me his blog post: "The three Finns are roughly the size of refrigerators except Yanni, the youngest, who is even bigger and has a striking resemblance to Lurch of the Addams family. They have distinguished themselves in the past by climbing Everest with no Sherpas. When they are not climbing, they are drinking vodka and Everest lager."

I laugh with Marshall, but I'm thinking that if I didn't have so much on the line here with my film I would be over there with them drinking vodka and talking about women too. They appear to be having way more fun than the rest of us. Apparently when Marshall met them the other day they asked him, "Why doesn't anyone ever write about climbing Everest drunk?" Of course this was just a joke—they don't bring booze with them when they climb the mountain. Their rest days at Base Camp, however, are a different story. They carry a small radio around camp, blasting the Beach Boys or the *Blues Brothers* soundtrack. One day I saw one of them doing dance moves to Aretha Franklin's "Think."

In marked contrast are the Good Finns: Mikka and Timo, both from northern Finland near the Arctic Circle. I met them in Asian Trekking's dining tent. Mikka sees the challenge of climbing like a business plan. In business you have to set your goal and split it up into steps. Climbing the mountain, he says, is the same. The difference between the Bad and the Good Finns, I decide, is like the difference between sexy late night jazz and sports bars, scarlet women and virgins. I would always choose the scarlet women. I prefer passion to economics.

After leaving Marshall, Andrew and I branch out to interview some other people. I have heard there is a small Canadian team set up about a hundred metres behind Asian Trekking's camp.

Before coming here, I hadn't realized how spread out Base Camp would be or, with over 1,000 people here, how impossible it is to speak to even a small fraction of them all. Choosing characters with only a two-person film crew has its challenges. It would be very difficult to follow someone who is an hour's walk away on the other side of Base Camp, for instance. Yet I very much want to follow a few different teams to get a sense of the different motivations. So I mentally draw a fifteen-minute radius from our camp and decide to seek out our characters from within that circle.

To get to the Canadian camp we cut across Asian Trekking's camp and go down a small ravine, which is dry now but will have a full-fledged river in it by the time we leave. As we scramble up the other side we see the Canada West Mountain School banner hanging on a big rock and a man in orange sport sunglasses smiling at us. He looks like a slightly taller version of Bono, only he's got short dark hair with a touch of grey and he's wearing a fleece hoodie covered in corporate sponsor badges.

Andrew and I introduce ourselves. Right away I feel a kinship with this man because it turns out he and the rest of the team are from BC as well. When we tell him what we're doing, Robert Hill says he's on a Seven Summits campaign titled "No Guts Know Glory" to raise awareness for intestinal disease as well as living life with an ostomy. "I have Crohn's disease," Rob tells us, explaining that it's a painful inflammation of the digestive tract that causes weight loss, diarrhea, nausea and vomiting. There's a huge stigma attached to it because it's associated with bathroom issues, "which somehow frighten people," he adds. "Who wants to talk about bowel activities? Unless you are sitting at Everest Base Camp, where it's commonplace," he laughs.

Andrew and I laugh too. It certainly seems that on these kinds of extreme adventures life is about eating and going to the bathroom. I can't imagine climbing this mountain with an ostomy bag, though. And I am impressed with Rob's courage, which doesn't come off as bravado but rather as humility and a commitment to help others who suffer as he does.

Rob says his quest for the Seven Summits began when he was in a business class in university and had to write a proposal. The exercise forced him to think about what he wanted to accomplish in life. "I grew up with heroes like Terry Fox and Rick Hansen, both of whom are also from BC, Canada, and I thought maybe I could be someone like that for people with intestinal diseases. I love being in the mountains. It just feels really natural, very comfortable for me, and what better soap box to stand on than on top of the world?"

Rob's first Seven Summits climb was Russia's Mt. Elbrus. On his second, at Mt. Aconcagua in South America, he got sick with a kidney infection and had to be hospitalized. While in hospital he met a kid with ulcerative colitis, and it was then that he realized his No Guts Know Glory campaign was about connecting with other people who have inflammatory bowel disease, not just about the mountains. "The quote we use is that it is not about climbing mountains; it is about moving them," Rob says.

He tells us his second attempt to climb Mt. Aconcagua was successful, and since then he has ticked off all but Everest. It's not his first time here. "I was here in 2008, and while waiting for the Icefall to open I ended up catching some sort of bug. Originally we thought it was a Crohn's flare-up, but it turns out it wasn't. Whatever I ingested was bad enough with my compromised digestive system to send me home. It was tough, but other climbers I know who have been up Everest have said, 'Rob, no one was hurt, no one was killed, and people summited on your team, so you had a successful climb.' But I knew I just had to get healthy and get back here. I don't let the disease define who I am."

Rob's team includes his friend John O'Shaughnessy, a fellow ostomy. John's role is to get Rob's story out, updating websites where he is blogging, putting up YouTube content daily and pushing that out through social media sites. The other climber in the group is Darrell Ainscough. Darrell isn't part of the Crohn's mission but he has paid Canada West Mountain School to guide him to the top. Their professional mountain guide is John Furneaux from Squamish, BC. After catching up on their rotation plan I ask John what he has learned through his experiences as a guide.

"I find when you are in the mountains, everything is really simple. All the problems that you come across, you just deal with. It doesn't matter if it is big or small. And when you go back to the real world, all the so-called big problems of life aren't so big anymore. And you realize how simple things can actually be. And it's great taking people into the mountains and showing them that—how crazy and chaotic life can be at home, but when you are in the mountains all you have is the moment, and when you get home what you thought was a big problem is not anymore."

John's philosophy reminds me of what I learned at Outward Bound decades ago. We all determine what we believe our limits are, and in many cases we set them too low. I remember at seventeen being on a month-long Outward Bound course with a heavy army-issue knapsack and, after hours of hiking, looking ahead at a mountain we were to spend the last hours of the day climbing. I sat down and said to myself, "I give up, that is just not possible, I can't do it." But because the people I was with carried on, so did I. One step at a time, I walked to the top. The elation and adrenalin rush of the achievement were intense. But more importantly, the realization that I could push myself to achieve more than what I thought possible changed my life.

In the words of Reinhold Messner, the first climber to do a solo ascent of Everest without oxygen: "We climb high to go deep inside."

That is why I go to the mountains. What I realize now is that it is easy to be a holy man alone on a mountain—not so much when you share the experience with thousands.

Before heading back to our camp Andrew and I decide to continue over the ridge to check in on the Himalayan Rescue Association and get an update. We find Luanne enjoying a break sitting outside in the sun with her shades on. After some chit-chat Andrew sets up the camera, and when I ask her for an update, she tells me they've seen over two hundred patients in three weeks. I'm surprised. "That's a lot of people considering there are one thousand people here, one in five."

"Yes, there have been times when we have had a lineup outside our tent with mild illnesses, or concerns about a cough, but just the other day we had a pretty dramatic rescue in the Icefall. We were contacted early in the morning by radio that there was a climber up there who had profound shortness of breath and blue lips. You don't need a medical degree to know he was in trouble. A number of teams came together, one contributed an oxygen mask, another an oxygen tank, and then a guide gave up his climb to escort him down, gave him some medication, stayed in contact with us, and saved this guy's life."

I realize it really is just luck that saves you up there if you get into trouble. The thin air and hypoxia affecting you are affecting everybody else on the mountain too. It takes the random kindness of many strangers to save just one person who starts to die up there. I wouldn't want to have to factor that into my contingency plans for dealing with a question of my own life or death high up on Everest.

On our way back to our camp, we stop to film the pile of garbage that has been collected so far in an effort to clean up the mountain—piles of nylon rope, gloves, and the remains of a helicopter that crashed at Base Camp in 2006. Childon says he was there when it happened. One wheel of the chopper missed the helipad, the whole thing slid off and the blade smashed into rock. "I ran right away down to see to the helipad, but nobody was having a problem. They were alive, not hurt. Only the petrol tank was broken and all the petrol was going out. This"—he points to the garbage—"is from that."

The garbage collection is part of a cash-for-trash program Dawa Steven started after he came here in 2007 and saw garbage from previous expeditions all over the place. Today's expedition companies are good about carrying out what they carry in. What's piled here is all the garbage from previous expeditions, dating back to the 1950s. Melting ice reveals old sins.

Back at camp, I transfer twelve P2 cards using solar power. Childon has some bad news for me. We've spent only eight days at Base Camp and have another thirty-two to go, but we have already used half of the fuel we brought for our generator. And I can't charge camera batteries from the solar panels. They are only good for laptops and hard drives. Fuck.

BODILY FUNCTIONS

DAY 9: APRIL 28

I wake up this time with a wicked sore lower back. I haven't had a bowel movement in a few days and am getting close to my moontime. Oh joy, oh bliss. I have never taken so many pills in my life: antibiotics for bacterial infection, pills for constipation, pills for diarrhea, Diamox for altitude and loads of Advil and such for headaches. So far, more agony than ecstasy.

I drag myself out of my sleeping bag and go through what is becoming my morning routine at the world's highest campground. I pull my Gore-Tex pants and warm down jacket from inside my sleeping bag. I sleep with them at my feet so they are warm when I slip them on over the long johns, t-shirts and sweaters I wear to bed. Then I pull out my bathroom bag. Once the small bowl of water arrives at my tent door, I wash my face, neck and hands. Next I brush my teeth. The water bottles I used as heating pads are also at the bottom of my sleeping bag—dangerous, because if they were to open up I would be sleeping in a wet bag, which wouldn't be much good for warmth. But if I didn't store them at my feet the water in them would be frozen into an ice block by morning. I rinse my mouth out with some drinking water and spit into the small bowl of now dirty water, then put the bowl outside the tent and put on my hiking boots. At this point my body is facing the tent door and my feet are just outside. Once my boots are on, it is a forward thrust on to hands and knees and a few careful steps to the narrow walking trail.

Not far behind my tent is the bathroom tent. I walk briskly to the scary narrow plastic tent and stand nervously on the loose rock piled around the blue bucket that I must crouch over to pee. It is much worse than an outhouse, which would have a deep hole in the ground and an elevated toilet seat. This is a bucket of human waste that will only be changed every twenty days or so. I have to hover inches above. In any regard, no loitering, I'm in and out as fast as possible then over to the dining tent where Thermoses of hot water and tea await Andrew and me. This morning weather rumours abound, and Childon says there could be summit attempts between May 6 and May 12.

Base Camp is a fascinating place, with many climbers aspiring to be the first in one way or another. An American woman named Cleo wants to be the first to climb both Everest and Lhotse in one season without oxygen. Two Finn women are competing to be the first woman from Finland to summit. Then there are the increasingly younger climbers who want to summit. I just want to last another thirty-one days and descend to guesthouses with a shower and toilet in my room. The descent will also be a relief to my body, the oxygen in my hemoglobin being at the low end of the scale. I need to stay grounded. I take more pills.

Yesterday, coming back to camp after a long day of filming, I tripped on an unstable rock and fell. I'm lucky to get just a few bruises and a sore wrist. This morning I heard there was an avalanche on the Tibetan side of Everest and three climbers are missing. One of them is an Asian Trekking client. Sobering. Very, very, sobering. And nobody is talking about it.

In the evening it starts to snow and is bloody cold. I get myself into bed early with a hot water bottle trying to chase another bad chill out of my bones. Tomorrow Andrew is going to hike back down to Gorak Shep with Childon and Bashista. I will hang out with Marshall monitoring the camp radio. I am finding it hard to get immersive with characters on an 80-acre campsite built on a moving glacier. The thin dark moraine covers ice and makes it very easy to wipe out.

DAY 10: APRIL 29

By morning the snow has stopped falling and the sun is out. The interior of my tent has dried out, the dining tent is toasty for breakfast and the solar panels are getting a good charge, so I have no problem transferring footage. It's my first time alone without Andrew, Childon and Bashista and I feel like a teenager whose parents have left for the weekend. After a few hours I go film some people descending from the Khumbu Glacier and then head over to the communication tent to hang out with Marshall and Arjun, our fearless young Indian hero.

I sit down with the camera balanced on my knee, frame the shot, and never look at it again. I just keep eye contact with Arjun and Marshall so we all forget about the camera and have a normal conversation.

"My daughter is into dance, and I know nothing about dance. I'm intimidated. I'm going to have to get a book or something," Marshall jokes.

"You are not supposed to intellectualize it," I say. "You are supposed to experience it, like painting."

"I don't know," Arjun says loudly. "I saw a picture of Matisse, *Women in the Bath*, and I'm like, 'What the hell? I could paint that!' And it sold for millions."

Marshall tells him, "You think you could, but I bet you can't."

We all laugh, but Arjun's youth and relative inexperience are a point of concern for the group. I ask him if he is mentally prepared for the summit push.

"I find it quite funny when people say they are preparing for the mountain," he says. "When I go up the mountain, in the morning I am too lazy to think of these things. I just think 'Okay, it's time to go up the mountain again, oh shit.' I don't find it that scary that you need to plan mentally for it."

Marshall says, "That's why people are worried about you, Arjun."

Arjun laughs this off. "It's funny. You know, Meagan said the mountain starts grabbing you from behind like a monster once you get up to 8,000 metres."

I decide to push him on his bravado a little. "What about the fact that there are over 250 dead bodies up there?"

"Actually," he says giggling uncomfortably, "you can see one body when you go from Camp One to Camp Two—the orange climber, below the Lhotse wall. He wasn't in good shape. At the time I thought it was fascinating and I zoomed in and took pictures, but that night it came back to me, and it wasn't good. I couldn't sleep. All I could see was the climber." He twists his upper body into the shape of the frozen climber. "I deleted that picture. At the time it didn't affect me but afterwards it did. They said when that climber was coming down, it was cloudy and he went the wrong way, fell down and died."

Talk of pictures of dead bodies brings back memories for Marshall. "When I was in Iraq, everyone would share really gruesome photos, usually on a memory stick. It was really weird and I don't know how it started. You would meet someone and you would chat for a while, and then you would say, 'Hey, do you want to trade pictures?' And we would trade pictures of blown-out bodies and stuff. I never kept any, but I always looked at them. Meagan and I were talking about it and trying to figure it out. I think I looked at them because I wanted to know what could happen to me and come to terms with it. I could see this guy blown up and I would think, 'Okay, that is the worst that can happen.' Is it the same way on the mountain when you see a dead body?"

Arjun shakes his head. "Actually, at that point in time you are having an adrenalin rush. You are excited. You have reached a new place. There are many things in your mind because you have to climb up, you have to come down, you have to take care of safety. You say, 'Okay, it is a dead body.' But after that, like in the night when I was in the tent, I was rolling around in my sleeping bag."

The conversation turns to other nightmares, such as having to pee in the middle of the night, and I think how quickly the conversation descends back to bodily functions when everyone's in survival mode. Arjun tells us the only time he feels homesick is when he has to get up at 3 a.m. for a leak. I tease him, asking if needing to pee makes him miss his mom.

"No, I miss my bathroom!" he says. "Here it is bad. At home you can hold it, but here, as soon as you feel it you have to run. Dawa was telling me, 'Please wear your shoes when you get up in the night to go to the bathroom, because you can get hurt.'"

People have died on Everest at Camp Three stepping outside to pee.

The tents there are like nests perched high up on a small ledge of a large vertical ice wall. To slip off the edge is to fall to your death.

The bathroom problem is something that happens to everyone at high-altitude: urination increases while the ability to hold it decreases. I make a mental note to research why that is. Many climbers in camp each have a pee bottle to help them deal with this problem. Neither Marshall nor Arjun is a fan of it. "I just used the pee bottle once at Camp Two, because it was freezing cold and I didn't want to get out of my sleeping bag," says Arjun.

"I still don't understand the mechanics," says Marshall. "I don't know how to pee in a bottle in my sleeping bag. I was in the room with Dawa Steven on the way up and he jumps up, and he has his headlamp on, and he is running around the room. He had spilled some, so he was trying to find wet wipes and just freaking out. And I thought, I don't even understand the angles, how that works to begin with."

Arjun agrees. "We have two bottles, one for pee, and one for water, and they are the same size, same shape and everything. There's just a colour difference, and at night you can't see that. So it's horrible in the night when you grab the wrong one and you pee in it and the next morning you can see the colour difference. It's bad."

I have yet to try peeing in a bottle but while filming in the high Arctic I tried using a cup with a hose affectionately called a pee funnel. I only used it once. The funnel sits in your underpants and you pull out the hose like a man pulls out his, so to speak. Then you pee standing up, which as a woman feels strange. The first few seconds worked fine; I stood there relieved I didn't have to undo suspenders and peel off my coat in minus forty degrees. Then I started feeling something warm dripping down my leg. Apparently the funnel can overflow if it's not tilted properly.

THE COLOMBIANS

DAY 11: APRIL 30

It is snowing heavily, and the weather forecast calls for three days of it. Blessed goddess, give me strength. I go to bed by 7:30 p.m. as I do every night, because it is the only place to knock the chill. Reading is difficult with big gloves but without them my fingers go numb in minutes. Writing is difficult too, for the same reason. I sleep in three sleeping bags. The outer bag is damp from nightfall until morning sunrise. If there is no sun it remains damp all day. The second, larger bag is the actual sleeping bag, rated to minus seventeen degrees Celsius. And then finally a flannel insert. Still, I get cold. On my head I wear a lined Nepali toque, around my neck a flannel scarf, on my top half a long-sleeved merino wool undershirt, a flannel shirt, a flannel pullover and a down jacket. On my bottom half I wear long fleece underwear, pants and thick wool socks.

Childon has come through and gotten us a satellite radio so I can monitor what is happening around camp. Every team has a radio and a channel, and given the size of Base Camp this is the only way I can know what is going on. I sleep with it next to my head so I can keep connected to my scattered characters. By day it sits on the kitchen table. Most teams keep their satellite radio on their own channel to monitor their clients on the climb but we flip through the channels, mostly listening in on Asian Trekking and the HRA. There are hundreds of these satellite radios at Base Camp—modern-day walkie-talkies with way better reception.

Today, Andrew brings news of the outside world, having just come back from Gorak Shep, where he checked the Internet. An oil rig in the Gulf of Mexico is spewing crude into the ocean, and there is ongoing political tension in Kathmandu. Andrew has also heard that we are not the only ones facing technical issues. Some web technicians from Toronto have equipment frying out. So, fingers crossed, we have twenty-nine more days to go. We are down to one working laptop, and in two days will exchange our hard drives for two new ones. Who knew technology could invoke so much fear?

Andrew and Bashista have already pulled out the map to look at the route back to Lukla. Because we arrived four days early they want to leave early. That isn't going to happen—we are here for forty days. I need to follow my characters and their stories until they succeed or fail on their summit attempts.

There are fluctuating reports as to when that might happen. Right now winds are blowing at 80 kilometres an hour on the peak and temperatures are minus thirty degrees Celsius. Meagan is at Camp Two and plans to push for Camp Three today. She got a weather update last night at 6 p.m., which I listened to on the satellite phone. It is windy up there, minus twenty-two and with snow expected.

This morning Apa left with Arjun, two other women from India and the two Finnish men for a rotation to Camps One, Two and Three. This is their third and final rotation before their summit push. Yesterday the Crohn's team from Canada went up.

With most climbers on the mountain, I have time to get some other story elements. Overall, I am physically and emotionally okay. We have reached the last day of April. It's been thirty days since we left home. I'm excited that tomorrow is the first of May, but I still don't have a film in the can. It's a terrifying thought, but I know I've just got to start the push. Base Camp can crack your psyche like a nut. I've got to stay positive. Positive makes positive. Make. Believe.

I get two minutes on the satellite Internet, which costs me twenty bucks. I use it to send a very brief "I am okay" email to Teresa. The more remote, the more expensive. Good rule for the modern entrepreneur.

I miss my home and am dying for a warm body to hold. The nights are so damn cold. And the idle time with the mind is an existential nightmare.

The question "why?" echoes in the darkness. Ego? Everybody here tells me they feel more alive when they are closer to death. Maybe if I can understand them, I can understand myself.

I heard a rumour today that the first summit push could be May 4, with winds of only 15 kilometres an hour in the forecast. I can't see my characters being ready for that window. For my part I've got to rev things up on the shooting schedule. Discipline is hard when basic human survival is on such a thin line. I tell myself again and again to stay positive, stay positive.

More avalanches crash and glaciers moan in the distance. Closer, coughing. Another verse of the Everest lullaby. I say a silent prayer.

DAY 12: MAY 1

Sometime in the middle of the night I wake up with a painful lower back. I drag myself out of my three sleeping bags and go for a pee. Just that act leaves me breathless, panting like an exhausted dog, but I am rewarded for my efforts by a starry sky with a big moon and clear peaks, beautiful and silent.

In the morning, the sun is shining and the threat of a three-day snowfall has vanished. I can hear our cook singing and open the tent door for some fresh air. It's been eighteen days since I've had a shower. My lower back is still sore, either from sleeping on ice on a half-inch of foam or because my period is coming. I keep telling myself that without pain there is no self-discovery.

I think of myself as a good person, but here I am reminded that not only am I selfish, but I also have a major case of Western entitlement. It is easy to take comfort for granted until you're sleeping on rock and ice with a sore back, shitting in a communal bucket and getting by with no running water. Unplug from Western domestic comfort and the psyche gets worked over. I'm calling it boot camp for the soul. The Buddhists have a saying: it is better to conquer yourself than to win a thousand battles. Since talking to Ani Choying I have come to realize that a major source of my energy is anger. It started in childhood. I was born in the 1960s when women were fighting for rights and becoming "liberated." Yet in 1970 a woman still could not be a policeman, fireman or professional hockey player. Actually, we still can't be professional hockey players. And we still have no spiritual equality in the world's major religions. So, like millions of other women, I have fought hard to be who I wanted to be. My attitude was, and still is, "Fuck you. Yes I can." Ani wants the same thing—equal opportunity for women—but she has found a way to do it without anger. Her way makes no enemies. Mine does.

Today we film the second-youngest character for the film, Bhagyashree Sawant. Bags is also a paying client of Asian Trekking. She is eighteen, from Mumbai, and has no climbing experience. Wearing a rainbow-coloured wool hat, braces on her teeth, an orange t-shirt and blue Gore-Tex pants, she stands with the Khumbu Glacier behind her and explains what brought her to Everest.

"When I was in grade four I read a chapter about Bachendri Pal, the first female Indian mountaineer to climb Mt. Everest. I never knew what mountaineering was but last year a girl from my state climbed Mt. Everest with Asian Trekking and that is when I found out it was being done this way. So I enquired into many companies but they said I needed more experience, because I have no mountaineering experience. Asian Trekking told me, 'We can train you.'

"In India I am good at sports. I am a national athlete, a national cyclist and rugby player. I know I am small but I am a good sprinter. I have good endurance. I am mentally prepared, but I don't know how to use the equipment."

Bags is studying computer science but thinks she may want to be a pilot. She tells me she skipped her grade twelve exams to be here. "My books were in front of me but my mind wasn't there. I talked my mom into it but the most difficult part was convincing my dad. He said to my mom, 'Have you gone mad? What are you doing? She is just a kid, don't let her do this—it is very risky.' So I stopped talking to my dad for a couple of days, pulled some tantrums, I won't eat this, I won't eat that… It is actually because of my mom [that I am here] because she always supports me and says, 'Go for it, what are you scared of?' What she believes is if you really want to do something, go for it. Don't give a shit what the world says.

"I just spoke to Meagan because I don't know about mountaineering. The only thing she told me is that you are very light and wind will be a problem for you." Bags laughs. "I am not worried about anything. It's my own choice."

It's hard not to be afraid for Bags. This morning I heard on the satellite radio that the Asian Trekking climber missing on the Tibetan side of Everest was confirmed dead. He was an experienced Hungarian climber named László Várkonyi. Apparently a serac collapsed and the ensuing avalanche swept him and the rope he was attached to into a crevasse, which then filled in with snow and ice debris.

I see why Apa is so stressed. Bags is one of his responsibilities. The dangerous thing about being able to buy any experience in the world is the false sense of security it gives people. After talking to Bags, Bashista leads Andrew and I to the tents of a small team from Colombia. I'm still looking for characters to bring into my film and Bashista has told me one of their climbers only has one leg. The idea of an amputee climbing Everest intrigues me.

The Colombian team arrived at the beginning of April. Their camp has many small plastic Colombian flags hanging from all their tents. They have already done three rotations, the last being just 100 metres short of Camp Three. They plan to descend to a lower village called Dingboche tomorrow for a week of rest, then will come back for a summit attempt. They want to be a little bit ahead of the others to avoid the traffic jam high on the mountain. They welcome the idea of being in the documentary and sign my release forms. Their team is small: six climbers and a woman named Carolina who is looking after their communications. They are partly financed by Colombian companies and their outerwear is covered with corporate patches—like most climbers here, they literally wear their financing on their sleeves. They've paid the $25,000 permit fee and have some Sherpas but not at the one-per-client ratio that Asian Trekking provides.

My character from this team will be Nelson Cardona Carvajal, the raison d'être of this expedition. He is in his fifties and speaks passionately in Spanish. I have no idea what he is saying until Carolina translates his words. What I see is a cool guy with shades and a bandana, speaking from his heart, here to climb the world's highest peak with only one leg. His other leg ends at the knee, to which is attached a metal rod in a shoe. He tells me he lost his leg in an accident while training for an Everest expedition in 2006.

"I literally flew down from an eighteen-metre wall and I had many open fractures. I broke my tibia, peroné [fibula], my coccyx was destroyed. I also had five maxillofacial fractures. I lost my teeth and I had a cranial fracture that took me to the edge of life and death."

It took two years for Nelson to recover from the accident. Doctors told him he could never climb or ride a bike again because his leg was too fragile and it would be too risky. "My essence—more than mountaineering—is practising sports," Nelson says, so he talked to Juan Pablo, who has always been the leader of Colombian expeditions, and said he would amputate his leg so he could go back into the mountains. Juan Pablo's answer was, "Well, you won't be in a beauty contest, you won't need to show your legs. You're an athlete, a mountaineer." A doctor standing next to them during this conversation argued, but Nelson persisted, and it was because of his persistence, he says, that he is here at Base Camp. "Gandhi said, 'Failures, defeats, reverses and tragedies are only experiences that precede success.' I am here for success," he adds with a big smile.

Standing next to Nelson and Carolina, Juan Pablo watches quietly. He also appears to be in his fifties, with a black beard and moustache and soft brown eyes. He first tried to climb Everest in 1997 with the first Colombian expedition. They didn't succeed, but when they came back in 2001 he was one of three Colombians to be the first from their country on the summit.

Carolina Ahumada Cala is beautiful. With long black hair and a warm smile, she moves with grace and is very kind. She is in charge of communication. Day by day she sends reports to the media in Colombia about what is going on with the expedition. This is the payoff for the sponsors.

Also camping out with the Colombian team is Albert Bosch, from a region in the north of Spain called Catalonia. Albert met the Colombian team here at Base Camp and will climb with them and share resources. He tells me he is writing a book, not about his adventures but for entrepreneurs. "In the chapters I define skills an entrepreneur must have that are similar to the adventure," he tells me.

I ask if he has a spiritual connection to the mountain.

"Not at all," he says. "The superstitions are useful for any community who needs them as energy, which I respect and support and everything, but the mountain is a rock."

Andrew is happy to hear Albert's perspective as it echoes his sentiments. He is a child of scientists, so most of the spiritual reverence of this mountain is superstitious nonsense for him. I don't see things so literally. As an artist I live in a world of metaphors and allegories. I do believe we have a soul. The first time I saw a dead body was when I went to the funeral of my grandmother. As I looked at her lifeless body and touched her cold skin, it hit me that our bodies are just suitcases. The spirit, the life energy of my grandmother animated her facial expressions, even held her body in a certain posture. Without that energy the body in the casket had no resemblance to her.

After an afternoon filming the Colombians and drinking some really good coffee, we head back to our dining tent. All is well until Andrew asks Childon if we can get a gas heater for our dinner tent. Every other team has one, he notes. Childon very kindly tells Andrew he will ask, but Bashista gives us this under his breath: "Don't ask for more. You got a phone, you got a generator, no heater."

I pay Asian Trekking for my camp services, not Bashista. Yet Bashista insulted Andrew by suggesting he was a spoiled Westerner for wanting something every other team has here but us. I feel as though the oversight is my mistake. I never requested a heater but I never knew such a thing was even an option. Regardless, Bashista's comments distress Andrew, who was offering to pay for a heater to be brought up by a porter or yak. Next, Bashista suggests that perhaps we are not receiving the best service from

Asian Trekking, and if I come again he could advise us.

It's a small moment, but I feel like a ship's captain with a mutiny brewing below deck. Just a rumble, but a rumble nonetheless.

Today I see a blackfly and a moth—the first insects I have seen at Base Camp. It must mean better weather, I think, and Bashista agrees it is a good sign. At night there is mercifully no snow, and although I can see my breath, I can't see ice crystals on the inside of my tent.

Strange place.

SNOWFALL

I wake up with the usual intense urge to pee. I open up my tent fly to a wall of snow. Mondo dump: about a foot on the ground, and it is still falling, remarkably silent. I am guessing walking around will be dangerous, with hidden crevasses and weak ice from the previous days' melts. I have a small headache again, and my body still feels sore. Middle-aged, high-altitude camping. I have twenty-seven days of filming ahead of me at Base Camp and I have not had a full day off for weeks. Fatigue is kicking in.

Although our camp is right next to the Kazakhstan team and our mess tent is maybe 5 metres from theirs, it has taken me a while to work up the nerve to walk into a tent full of Russian-speaking men to ask if they will be in the documentary. As I do, the first thing I see is meat hanging from the walls, then a mess of porn magazines, chocolate bars and bottles of what I discover is homemade vodka on the table. As well there are packages of vacuum-packed horsemeat, apparently a real Kazakhstan delicacy. The captain of the team is Max, who speaks some English. The team consists of six people: three with lots of experience and three who are attempting their first-ever ascension of an 8,000-metre peak. Their next excursion is to summit Lhotse. Kazakhstan just recently got independence from Russia, so the purpose of their mission is to use these climbs to help build nationalism and pride in their country. After having a shot of vodka and a toast—which is what you do when you walk into a Kazakhstan tent—Andrew and I film Max, who speaks in Russian and broken English. It isn't till I get to Canada that I get his interviews translated. I don't find it all that difficult to follow the gist of his words, as I lost over half of my hearing years ago and am used to piecing together sentence fragments with body language.

Max tells us that the Kazakh national mountaineering team has climbed thirteen peaks that are higher than 8,000 metres above sea level. Lhotse is the final peak remaining before they complete "this nationally significant plan" to climb the fourteen highest peaks in the world. This is the team's second attempt to climb Lhotse. Weather disrupted their plans the year before. Sadly one of their teammates died on that expedition, and three days ago they found his body below Camp Three. After they climb Lhotse they plan to try and bring their friend's body down for a proper burial.

After leaving the Kazakh team, Andrew and I split up to film separately. Andrew films B-reel of the camp in snow. Climbers at the Asian Trekking camp are playing around and laughing. Bags is having her first snowball fight with the staff and kitchen guys. The mood today is good. In stark contrast, I find Marshall sitting in his yellow one-man tent looking worried. He tells me the snow has thrown a few kinks in their plans. They have a lot of people at Camp Two who had planned to go to Camp Three today but can't move forward or back because of the snow. One of their Finn members, Timo, is sick. He intended to come down, but is also stuck at Camp Two. And Marshall has just had a weather report showing that we are in for more snow. "I am pretty concerned about it," he says. "I don't want anybody to be stuck up there at Camp Two. They are just losing energy but they can't go to Camp Three, so they are not acclimatizing, which makes me really nervous. I am just worried that what is an uncomfortable situation today will become a very dangerous situation tomorrow."

As I leave Marshall I bump into Bags, who has just finished her frolic in the snow and wears the smile of a child at a playground, but is similarly concerned about the snow. "My name means fortunate," she says. "But with this weather, I am not fortunate. I couldn't go on the first rotation because I got dizzy in the Icefall, so had to start after most of the team. This time they are on their third rotation and I am still stuck here waiting for my second. So my fortune is going on a roller coaster."

It is hard to believe that a young woman who has never been to a mountain and who has never seen snow is having her first experience of both here at Everest. Jesus, I hope she is fortunate. More snow expected over the next few days is worrisome; fresh snow hides the dangers underneath.

I meet a Sherpa climbing with a group of Koreans who tells me that he lost his toes as a child while working as a porter. He wants to work for two more years as a climbing Sherpa and then open a trekking company and bike touring business. It's a job for him. The Sherpas try to keep a sacred respect alive, but ultimately, this is a business. If I compare it to our commercialization of nature at places like Whistler, BC, close to my home in Canada, it puts things in perspective. If we commercialize the mountains where we live by turning them into ski resorts, how can we judge the Nepalese for commercializing mountains here in Khumbu?

After filming, Andrew and I return to our orange Marmot dome tent, aka our office/mess tent, to find Bashista in a happy mood. He has grown a beard since coming to camp and is wearing a black wool hat and a black North Face jacket. He tells us the government offices in Kathmandu are all being block-aded by the Maoists today. "Maybe we make a new government in Nepal. I think so," he says, telling us that sixty-five members of the country's coalition government crossed the floor to the Maoist side. "Today, nobody opens their shops in Kathmandu. Nobody goes to work in the government."

I ask him if the people of Kathmandu are scared. "Yes," he says. "Maybe violence now." At this, he dances around like a happy Hindu leprechaun, making me think he must be a Maoist himself. "Bashista, this is the happiest I have seen you since we left Kathmandu."

"I like so, sure. I don't like India or America, Canada. I like China."

Ta da: for all that second-guessing since meeting this guy in Kath-mandu, my gut instinct was right. He is not our friend. "Why? Tell me why? Why is China better than India, Canada and America?"

Bashista replies with a shit-eating grin, "No, no," and he laughs. "No, no, no, I am not a politician. I say no more."

He doesn't need to. Neither do I. And then his phone rings and the happy Hindu leprechaun prances away toward his tent.

I find out the ring I just heard is a historic one. Today is a first for cellular phone coverage at Base Camp. A transceiver tower has been erected and activated at Gorak Shep. When Bashista comes back to the dining tent after his phone call he tells me he no longer cares that we go back sooner. Now he is joking that six months at Base Camp is okay.

DAY 14: MAY 3

The sun is out. Yesterday's snow is still everywhere. With so many climbers at Camp Two, Base Camp is quieter than it was a week ago. I'm not sure of the status of all the climbers. I expect to see some of them back today while some will push to Camp Three. I'm very weak. Everything takes effort. We spend the morning filming some B-reel and transferring footage, which leaves us both feeling wiped out, so we withdraw for a little midday tent time.

Twenty-six more days of filming here. Part of me thinks that having spent seventeen days at high-altitude with no serious problems means I must be acclimatizing okay. The other voice in my head wonders what might be happening inside my body, beneath the surface. Being responsible for your life up here is a precarious dance with fate. It's like the classic story of the climber who pushes to the top but doesn't think about getting back down and dies on the descent. I don't want that to be true of filmmakers as well. One day at a time. The mountains look beautiful. I resolve to stay positive.

Our Kazakh neighbours bring us chocolate and smoked horsemeat. I pass on the horsemeat. The chocolate is from Almaty, their hometown, and that I have no problem with.

UPDATE FROM JOHN AND THE CANADIAN MEN

The Canadian men have a very homey kitchen tent—square, rather than dome-shaped, with tables covered with tablecloths running along the side walls. Pink plastic flowers serve as centrepieces on a table in the middle of the room. Strung across the back wall is one of those fuzzy tinsel strings usually found on Christmas trees.

I've taken to thinking of the two men named John on the Canadian team as "Guide John" and "Comms John" (for communications). Today Guide John is in faded jeans, a black hoodie, a red down vest and white-rimmed square shades with orange-tinted lenses. Buglike. He is in good spirits: his clients have just finished their third rotation. He says yesterday's 76 centimetres of snow made coming down to Base Camp more challenging. "From Camp Two to Camp One, you are in a big white glacier with big white walls," Guide John explains. "There is nothing to focus on so if your navigation isn't practised, you could be wandering around the big white bowl and getting lost. That was the challenging part. Once in the Icefall the snow actually helps a bit. The UV gets absorbed by the snow, instead of the ice, so it makes it more stable."

"However, fresh snow also covers up crevasses," I add.

"That is why it is good not to go first," Guide John laughs. "There is a pretty well-established trail, and there is a fixed rope through 90 percent of the Icefall, so it gives you a good path to follow. But the Icefall is changing daily so sometimes that path has changed, and you have to find a new way around crevasses that have just opened up. For the most part it is fairly easy to follow."

The Sherpas, he explains, are carrying supplies to Camp Four on the South Col, the high camp that most climbers stay at before their summit push. He says from Camp Two if you look at the Lhotse face there are 150 Sherpas going up the South Col every day. "Most of them will be carrying tents and oxygen, carrying anywhere from 15 to 45 kilos. It's amazing the difference, the strength of Sherpas, the speed of the Sherpas. I wouldn't bring clients here without using local support. The cooking staff keep you healthy, well fed, and provide great Base Camp services," he says, sweeping his hand around the room. "And the Sherpas are key. We have three Sherpas, one-to-one for the climbers. We are essentially climbing the mountain with a day pack, so the Sherpas are doing the majority of the carrying of oxygen, food, tents, everything. We have a tent like this at Camp Two. It's all about using your energy on the climb, and relaxing when you are in camp."

I tell Guide John I don't think all guide companies are created equal.

In fact, they vary a lot in terms of the services they offer, the fees they charge, and the quality of their provisions.

"Some companies just offer logistics and support, so they are not providing Western mountain guides," he explains. "They are saying, 'Here's a camp, there's a mountain, here's a Sherpa, have fun.' With our company, Canada West, I am the mountain guide, I climb with the climbers, spending all my time with them, making the safety decisions on the mountain at all times; whereas climbers with other companies might just have radio contact and support. Hopefully people know what they are getting into."

I mention Asian Trekking and how they were willing, for $45,000, to take eighteen-year-old Bags up the mountain, when she has never been on a mountain or even seen snow before.

"Yes, every company has different prerequisites," he says. "Most people are just happy to take your money. There are people who make it through the Icefall and turn around and go home, and then their guides just pocket the money. Our company does heavy-duty screening. This is my second trip here, and I wouldn't take clients I didn't know. On a trip of this scale I would have to have a history with those people. Both Rob and Darrell are people I have climbed extensively with."

With Guide John's experience on other Asian mountains, I ask him how Everest Base Camp compares with base camps on other mountains. His answer surprises me. "Everest Base Camp is like staying at the Hyatt. Base camp at K2 in Pakistan is like staying in a three-star hotel. Here it's easy to get supplies, and easy to get low. You can walk down to the lower villages here, where in Pakistan you are walking for a week on a glacier with no sign of anybody. Nepal has the logistics very dialed, and it is easy to be comfortable."

Leaving the Canadians' camp, as I stumble over rocks and ice, jump a small glacial stream, and huff and puff my way back to our home base, I beg to differ about this being like any Hyatt I have ever stayed at. My imagination slips into a vivid fantasy about white sheets, a hot shower and a nice clean bathroom. At that very moment my foot breaks through the ice crust and plunges into a stream of icy water. You want to learn how to be in the moment? Forget yoga, come to Everest Base Camp.

HIGH-ALTITUDE MEDICINE

DAY 15: MAY 4

My day starts with a treat: my first bowl bath. The sun is out, so Miloh boils a big pot of water, pours it into a large bowl for me, and places it on the rock and ice in our skinny black shower tent erected weeks ago for this purpose. I think this is the first time anyone in the group has used it. Andrew has taken the time in the morning to wash his body after washing his face in his tent with the small hand bowls of water we get every morning. But the mornings, if the sun is shining, are the only times I feel warm, so the idea of taking off my clothes to do the same hasn't appealed to me. I generally have a face and hand wash, brush my teeth, and get on with the day. We are sort of like the odd couple from the 1970s Neil Simon sitcom about two divorced guys who live together. Andrew is Felix, the clean and tidy one. I'm Oscar, messy and unshaven.

But today I'm going to change that. The floor of the shower tent, like every surface here, is cold, sharp granite. The surface is uneven and the large silver bowl full of hot water is carefully balanced on top of a few stones. I take off my clothes but keep my hiking boots on because the ground is too cold to stand on. Having spoken to Marshall, Arjun and Meagan about their techniques, I know there is a method to the bowl bath. So I squat next to the bowl and wash my face first, then dip my head in to get my hair wet. Next I shampoo my hair, then dip and rinse my head in the bowl. After that, using a cloth, I wash my body. It's hard to say how much weight I have lost. My legs look thinner and maybe my stomach is flatter. And somebody stole my tits. They were much larger when I got here.

Meagan has just come down from her final rotation, so Andrew and

I film her sitting outside her tent. She is frustrated because their team received conflicting weather reports again and she got nailed by a snowstorm. While the heavy snowfall didn't make her climb any more difficult, coming down was another issue. The weight of the snow on the ladders through the Icefall had loosened many of them. The ice doctors will have a lot of work to do. Meagan says if she is on the mountain when snow falls she likes to let everything settle for a day before coming down. That is a good one to remember.

With his mind still on the conversation about a heater for our dining room tent, Andrew asks Meagan about the amenities at Camp Two.

"Camp Two is actually quite a decent place," Meagan says. "It's very much like Base Camp. We have our tents. There is a mess tent and a cook tent. There seems to be all kinds of food at the cook tent. One of the members of our team wanted whole-wheat chapatti, not white chapatti and they made him some. They had whole-wheat flour, go figure. In our mess tent where we eat, they had a carpet on the floor and they had tables and chairs, and they had all the condiments you could really want—soy sauce, ketchup, salt and pepper, whatever."

Andrew asks, "Yes, but is there a heater in the dining room up there?"

Meagan and I laugh and Meagan repeats that it's much like Base Camp, then tells us that from Camp Two you can see the Lhotse Face, which looks like it has a line of ants crawling up it.

"It's weird: when I look at the Lhotse Face it seems like all of Base Camp is climbing Mt. Everest at the same time and heading for Camp Three, but at Camp Two it is very secluded. You don't have a sense of how many people are there. You really just spend your time at Camp Two with your Camp Two people. Very rarely is there socialization."

That's true of Base Camp too. For the most part people don't socialize. That surprised me at first, but at this altitude there is no wood for a fire, and fire is what gathers people. But I think another reason is that people don't want to get sick. All the training and all the money and then getting here and all the waiting, the most important thing is not to get sick. And judging by the chorus of nighttime coughing I hear in the Everest lullaby, there are a lot of people at Base Camp fighting the Khumbu cough.

I ask Meagan how people pass the time at Camp Two.

"If you have finished your book in the first two days like I did, you spend it staring at the walls of your tent. Honestly, I wish I could say I was kidding, but the snow was falling and it made shadows on the walls so I made pictures out of them and I made stories." Laughing, she shakes her head. "I am not even kidding. I wish I was. I mean, I wrote in my notebook, but there is only so much of that you can do. And of course you're also just focusing on the climb ahead."

At this point Arjun comes over with a cup of tea. He too has just come down from his final rotation. "We started climbing and there was sudden snowfall. I wasn't wearing the right clothes and my hands were cold. I was briefed, anything happens to you, just tell your Sherpa. So I told my Sherpa, and he came and rubbed my hands, which felt really good."

He smiles at my raised eyebrow and carries on: "The climbing to Camp One was really good, but it gets a bit tiring after that. You can see Camp Two but like, so near, so far. At Camp Two we spent four days. It was very bad. You spend hours in your tent, then they yell, like your mom when you're a kid, 'Okay, lunch is ready.' It's only ten yards away but you breathe heavy and you feel exhausted by the time you reach the mess tent. But I like it. Some people like drugs and alcohol—I like this. I like testing my limits. Every time I go out there I have to say in my head, 'Come on, come on, one more step, two more steps. Okay, come on, come on.' I like that."

At this point, with a near-chronic head- and backache, the drugs and alcohol sound better, much better. Arjun also says that their weather reports were incorrect, so when the winds reached almost 100 kilometres per hour, they weren't prepared, and he and his Sherpa guide decided to descend.

"I was actually pretty scared—that was the first time I ever experienced bad winds. While going up the Lhotse Face, I puked. I felt better after that. It was a relief, and I thought I was feeling better so I could continue. But then I got worse, my body got exhausted and I had a bit of fever. So we came down."

We say goodbye to Arjun, then venture under sunny but windy skies over a few small hills of moraine and ice back to the HRA for another update. Today we talk to Dr. Steve Halvorson, an American. He wears a black Everest ER baseball cap with a white plastic flower. We set up outside the tent, where I ask him to tell us about the things that are happening inside the body at high-altitude.

"First of all, no matter what you do, your body is dumping a great deal of fluid."

As he says this I have an *aha* moment, thinking of sitting back at camp, looking over the barren terrain and watching people sprint to the bathroom tents.

Steve continues, "It is common for people to lose quite a bit of weight strictly in fluid. And secondly, your body is also stimulated to produce more red blood cells. Blood becomes thicker. Sometimes this can become a problem with clotting or sludging and not getting enough oxygen to parts of your body that need it. We also start producing chemicals that start travelling around in your blood, [to] help you grab oxygen from your lungs more efficiently and transport it to your tissues. The blood pressure can go up, your heart is pumping harder, which can cause cardiac arrest. The basis of it all is that the chemistry of your blood changes and becomes more acidic, so the kidneys kick in to help balance the body's pH. Your kidneys manage your electrolytes, and you can have extreme fluctuations in your electrolytes. Your heart doesn't like that too much and it can go into a fatal rhythm."

"So basically I'm dying, and if I have any unknown heart defects, prolonged exposure here will kill me?" I ask. Steve just nods his head. This is a sobering thought for me and my only crew member with his backwards heart.

Next we move inside the HRA tent to meet the famous Dr. Peter Hackett. Peter is considered the father of high-altitude medicine as he was one of the first to study why climbers at high-altitudes were complaining of the same ailments. He has just arrived at Base Camp and will be spending a few weeks here. He is wearing a red Everest ER jacket and has one of those weathered, handsome faces like Robert Redford's. I'm guessing he is much older than he looks. He lives in Telluride, Colorado, and has been doing high-altitude research for thirty-six years, ever since he first came to Nepal in 1974. I am excited he has agreed to be in the film.

Andrew and I set up the cameras, and I begin by asking him how he got started. He speaks so well and so thoroughly that Andrew and I, for the most part, just sit and listen, fascinated for the next ten minutes.

"Initially I was a rock climber, a trekker and an outdoors person and right after medical school at twenty-six I became a helicopter rescue doctor in Yosemite. I rescued a fellow by the name of Leo Labahn. Actually, I consulted him on his broken ribs that he injured climbing, and he needed a doctor in Nepal for three months. He owned a trekking company called Mountain Travel. It sounded great to me. He handed me a big, thick airplane ticket and after about fifteen stops I ended up in Kathmandu in the fall of 1974. Trekked up here to Everest region and I was surprised by how many trekkers got this virus with headaches, trouble sleeping, and a lack of energy, and when I got back down from the trek I realized, you know, that must be high-altitude sickness. And I started studying about it. There was very little known, and I thought this was really intriguing and a great opportunity to combine my medical profession with my passion for being in the mountains."

Peter spent the next few years helping to get the Himalayan Rescue Association started and took over as director from 1975 until 1982, living in Nepal most of that time. During that period he conducted and published a major study of the effects of Diamox (still the main drug used to combat altitude sickness), and in 1981 joined the American Medical Research Expedition on Everest. "In those days, there was one expedition per season allowed by the ministry of Nepal. So it was about twenty of us. Our purpose was to study physiologic function all the way to the summit. We had a research lab here at Base Camp and a research lab at Camp Two on the Western Cwm. It was a very successful mission. And I managed to go to the summit on October 24, which still might be the latest autumn summit, I'm not sure, and I had to do it alone from the South Col, without any ropes, because my Sherpa had to turn around. He thought his toes were freezing. So that was an epic for me, falling down the Hillary Step on the way back, nearly died, managed to drag myself back to camp. So I have a very special and unique relationship to this mountain. It almost killed me, I should say I almost killed myself on it and yet, it was obviously quite different in those days."

Peter's voice is slow and calm; he speaks with the humble authority of a wise elder. "I wouldn't recommend going to the summit alone, also wouldn't recommend waiting in a line for two hours to get to the top which is what happens these days. So things have of course changed. But what hasn't changed is that Everest is still a physiologic and medical problem more than it is a climbing problem. Climbers have to climb 11,500 feet (3,505 metres). That's all, from Base Camp to the summit. And if the base of the mountain was the same as Juneau, Alaska, sea level, and the summit read 11,500 feet, it probably wouldn't even be a popular climb. It wouldn't be one of the biggest mountains in Alaska for sure. But what makes it so unique is that climbers are putting themselves in a low-oxygen environment, which produces a lot of stress that normally we don't experience at lower altitudes. So acclimatization becomes crucially important, staying healthy is crucially important, and not everybody has the kind of genes that allows them to function at high-altitude. Some people are very good, fast acclimatizers; others can never acclimatize. It is a bell-shaped distribution and most of us are in the middle."

Clearly my genes do not like high-altitude. I live at sea level, as have generations of my Irish, French and Mi'kmaq heritage. I am like a fish out of water up here, and listening to Peter puts that clearly into perspective. I am on the back end of the bell curve.

"What really matters in terms of bringing out one's disposition is how much time you take. So the rate of ascent up the mountain becomes critically important. As a basic illustration, if I have a group of people at sea level and I take them to the summit of Mt. Everest in a huge helicopter, they will all go unconscious in two minutes. And yet, there are all sorts of climbers going to the summit this time, some with oxygen, some without.

They are not going to go unconscious—in fact, they are going to continue to walk and talk on radios and do blogs and function fairly well, although of course not feeling 100 percent. So that process of the body being able to adjust to low oxygen is called acclimatization. And the key is genetics and time. The Sherpas have unique abilities because they have been born at higher altitude and have larger lungs. But some of their ability is because of genetic adaptation. They are originally from Tibet. Tibetans have been living in high-altitudes we think for 50,000 years, so they have had time to adapt. When they get above 8,000 metres, they can still get HAPE or HACE. But there is no question that because of their evolution at high-altitude they have developed a number of mechanisms that make them superior to Westerners when it comes to high-altitude climbing."

Peter tells us more about Diamox, how in four hours it does what the body does in four days at high-altitude. In 1976, he helped establish Diamox as the best remedy to treat altitude sickness. I am grateful for it—I took it faithfully twice a day the first week we arrived and I know it helped, but regrettably it works less well over time.

As we wrap up our interview, we hear a helicopter coming in. It being a clear day, we pop out to get a wide shot of the helicopter coming into Base Camp. As it is landing, Peter says, "This is interesting. This is something you would never see in the old days." He tells us it's someone who flew out to Kathmandu for a few days' break, then got sick when he came back—from something he had in Kathmandu, not the altitude. So now he's flying out again.

The helicopter, without even turning off its engine, just touches down to pick up the climber and takes off again.

I ask Peter what he thinks is best—to drop lower for a few days or to stay here.

"I would like to do a study on that," he says, and pauses a moment before continuing. "In the old days, you would come back to Base Camp and that is as low as you would go. You wouldn't want to lose any acclimatization. My personal bias is that going down is psychologically great, warm and green, but I don't really think it makes much difference. This is low enough. You can acclimatize well enough here and if you go down you could miss the summit days. The weather could change. I think you want to stay around and be ready to move. Change the plans if necessary."

We head back to our camp for dinner. The guys are constantly trying to get me to eat more, but the palate is strange at this altitude. I crave certain foods. I could eat pappadums all day—have always enjoyed them, but now more than ever. I want popcorn, and toast with peanut butter, but have no desire for meat, eggs or cheese. I feel bad for the cook. He takes my unfinished meals seriously, like he's not doing his job. Tonight he made momos, which are fried dumplings. I liked them at 3,600 metres, but here not so much. Thankfully Andrew does and I can pawn off mine to him so Miloh's feelings don't get hurt again. The vacuum-sealed horsemeat is still sitting on our kitchen table right next to two large Thermoses, one filled with hot water and one with tea. I mix some orange-flavoured vitamin C crystals into a cup of hot water and call it dinner.

MAOIST REBELS

The Maoist rebellion has shut down government offices in Kathmandu. We are hearing stories that Lukla is packed with trekkers opting to stay there while the city is in disarray. There are no taxis, so there is no way of moving around. I don't know how the situation will unfold over the next three weeks.

DAY 16: MAY 5

By 5 a.m. light is creeping into the sky although the sun has not yet risen. There appears to be more fresh snow on the ground. My back is stiff like the ice I am sleeping on, and I'm on the second day of my period so I pop my daily Advil, which takes the edge off. I'm practising daily pain control.

The sky was full of lightning last night, flashing in the distance without thunder. It's odd to be eye level with the top of a lightning bolt, a reminder of how high we are. This morning the wind is ripping—it sounds like a 747 landing on top of us, making it hard to get any audio even with a wind boom.

I interview Apa in his tent. He says when you see a cloud that looks like a mushroom over Everest that means it is not good weather. And yesterday on the mountain he saw the cloud. "Normally I only spend two nights at Camp Two, but this last time we spent four nights. That is too much. But I had to do it. I tried to send my clients to Camp Three for sleeping one night to acclimatize but unfortunately the weather was not good. We should not spend that long on the mountain because we will lose our energy. So that's enough acclimatization. Now we just wait for the summit weather."

HANES

In addition to the many individuals who come to Everest for personal reasons, companies also come here to help brand their outdoor gear. Hanes is sponsoring a Canadian climber, Jamie Clark from Calgary, Alberta, to go up Everest to test some of their new gear. They are also handing out free buffs and hats, an act of what I like to call shameless self-promotion. I am somewhat reluctant to film them, not wanting my art to be their ad, but their presence here feeds right into my theme of the commercialization of Everest. So we walk over to their camp and talk to Mike Abbott, director of research and development for Hanes. I ask him if they have learned anything so far in product testing on Everest.

"Little things, pocket placement just needed to be tweaked. With their climbing harness on and a backpack, traditional pocket placement didn't work for the climbers. They couldn't reach them."

He tells us about a sock they've designed for cold weather that absorbs moisture and stores body heat in liquid capsules embedded in the yarn that release the heat back to the body when it starts to cool off. From the socks he talks us through the long underwear, the soft shell pant, the soft shell jacket, everything designed to take moisture away from the body.

After filming Mike inside a very warm dome tent that has us all in a full-body sweat by the time we leave, we set up outside to film the team's climber. Jamie Clark owns an outdoor store in Calgary. This corporate adventure is a partnership he has with Hanes to help them make a line of clothing, from base layer to top layer, using new materials and new designs. He tells us he's been here before and that it took three attempts to make his first summit.

"We have a small team, five highly skilled Sherpa climbers, our cameraman, Scott Simple, from the United States, and myself. This is my fourth Everest expedition. I was here on the north side in 1991 and 1994. Last time I was climbing on Everest was 1997. I was lucky enough to stand on the top back then. This time we want to test new clothing. We want to inspire the people who work at Hanesbrands and we want to inspire the consumer, the people who use this stuff."

Jamie goes on to explain that corporate sponsorship has always been a part of climbing Everest. And he says what he and Scott are doing is similar to what Mallory and Irvine did—they, too, were a small team with Sherpa support, climbing the mountain to bring prestige to their financers. The members of Jamie's team have completed their acclimatization hikes and are now waiting for a summit push, something he describes as "finding a balance between patience and urgency." His plan is to leave on May 8 and summit on May 12.

For some contrast to all of this new gear and corporate money, I split from Andrew and Bashista and head back over to Meagan's tent. Having the right gear is critical in any climbing expedition. Keeping it in good shape is also a challenge. I find Meagan in her tent, trying to sew her boots back together with a needle and thread. She ripped a boot with her crampon while ice-climbing up the Lhotse Face on her last rotation and has been holding it together with duct tape. After sewing the tears, she puts glue on all the new seams and uses a file to sharpen her crampons. "Did you hear we got cell service up here?" she asks with a shake of her head. "Jesus."

"Yup," I reply, joking that the next thing will be a ski lift to the summit.

I've learned a few things about Everest since we got here. I know, for instance, that once climbers get past the ice seracs and the sun and the sheer ice on the Lhotse Face, they have to climb the Hillary Step. That's where Peter Hackett said he almost died, and it's where people are often stuck in a bottleneck of climbers waiting to go up. So I ask Meagan to explain what the Hillary Step looks like and why it is so dangerous.

"You have the South Summit and the actual summit, and the Hillary Step is somewhere in-between. It's this ridge with a 2,400-metre drop on one side and a 3,000-metre drop on the other side. The Hillary Step is like a small cliff on the ridge, a very small bookcase type of a cliff. If a person were to fall coming down, they would have very little room for error. It is a very precarious spot. You have to own every step up there—you have to have strong legs. There's no room for tripping or stumbling."

I ask Meagan if she has heard that the Maoist rebels are heading to

Base Camp with guns, looking to extract money from all of us and for some international media attention. She says if they show up, she is going straight up to Camp One or Two so they don't fuck with her summit attempt. Clearly I am in need of a plan myself. I didn't get the memo before I arrived that I should budget for extortion. There are moments here when I feel like the horse in the Alex Colville painting running on the railway tracks toward a distant oncoming train.

Later, I speak with Bashista about it, and something about him makes me feel uneasy. He seems a little shifty. He tells me maybe I should give some money to the rebels if they ask for it. Andrew agrees. He, too, is anxious.

After dinner I hike back up a small slope to the Asian Trekking communication tent where I find Marshall. He lets me try to send an email to the Canadian embassy to let them know we are here. That turns out to be impossible. But I am able to send an email to Asian Trekking's office in Kathmandu to ask if they can look into earlier flights in case the political unrest escalates.

Meagan walks in while I am sitting there and laughs when I tell her I tried to contact the Canadian embassy. "Why are you doing that? They can't help you," she says, still smiling.

If things go wrong here with the Maoists, I have decided Marshall and Meagan are who I want to be with. Their military training is a really good thing. Meagan tells me the Canadian army does not have any resources to help us here if shit hits the fan. The only country that has the resources and has been known to go that mile for their citizens is the United States.

Tomorrow I need to hide and split hard drives.

DAY 17: MAY 6

I am not sure how concerned I need to be about the Maoist situation. I don't want to worry needlessly, but I also don't want to be without a plan, so I go looking for an update from Marshall and find him in the Asian Trekking mess tent hanging out with Bags. He tells me that Dawa Steven has been in touch with him and says it is calm in Kathmandu and has been completely non-violent so far. Even if the Maoists come up to these parts, he is sure it would be really laid-back, which makes me feel somewhat better.

Bags has just come back from a rotation. She says it took her nine hours to get to Camp One, where she rested for a day. It takes most people four hours. "After we got to Camp One my Sherpa made me a nice dal bhat because I was very hungry," she tells me. "The next day we went to Camp Two. It took me five hours. I asked my Sherpa, 'What am I going to do? I am so slow.' He said going slow on the mountain is not a problem. [But] on our way down through the Icefall I wanted to take pictures but my Sherpa was like, 'Keep moving, keep moving, it is very dangerous here. Move slowly but keep moving.'"

Bags has picked up a dry cough, and says that her throat was swollen at Camp Two. She admits that she feels exhausted. I can't judge her for that because I am feeling the same way. My eyes are puffy. I look and feel tired, and I get breathless walking anywhere in Base Camp.

I thought I would eventually get used to the diminished air supply up here, but I have not. When you look up at the sky, you think there is so much of it, so much oxygen, all the way up into the universe. Up here you realize how thin the breathable air around the planet is, and you think about all the pollution that we constantly throw into it. I decide it's no wonder everybody is dying from cancer.

Later, I hang out with Arjun. With his army fatigues and red baseball cap and glacier shades, he's looking like India's version of Justin Bieber. This kid is cool. His name, he tells me, comes from ancient Indian mythology. Arjun was a prince and an archer, both jobs requiring the ability to focus. I find it interesting that the two youngest people are both from India. Arjun stands with his hands in his pockets looking up at the Icefall under a clear and windy sky. When he turns back he says, "The weather is not good. Jet streams are coming in. Seventy, eighty miles per hour—not good. You see those small clouds? Very fast winds."

"How can you tell?" I ask.

Throwing his hands in the air as if he is shocked by my ignorance, he says loudly: "THAT'S SUBLIMATION—solid snow turning into straight clouds. You need very fast winds for that. That was like grade nine."

After laughing I ask him when he is thinking of going for the summit.

"I don't know. I just go when Apa goes. I don't know what's up with that guy, but whenever he goes on the mountain the weather is good."

Apparently not all the time, as Apa just spent four days stuck in snow at Camp Two. Still, Arjun has a point. If I were climbing Everest I would want to do it with Apa—can't argue with nineteen successful summits.

Arjun tells me that Conrad Anker visited the Asian Trekking team last night to show them some older photos of the Icefall. Anker is here working for National Geographic. Apparently the pictures reveal that the Icefall, which was already a dangerous place, has melted drastically and is now even more dangerous. Even I have noticed a big shift between 2007 and 2010.

Conrad Anker is an American mountaineer and a bit of a local legend here at Base Camp. He found Mallory's body on Everest in 1999 after retracing the route Mallory and Irvine took in their fatal attempt to summit in 1924. It was hoped that a camera would be found with Mallory's body to prove or disprove that he had reached the summit before he died. Because his goggles were found in his pocket it is assumed he was probably coming down the mountain at night, which could suggest he had made the summit, but most people still believe he never made it up.

This year Anker is here as part of an extreme ice survey researching the melting of the world's glaciers. His job is to mount five time-lapse cameras in three locations to document the changing glacial landscape on Mount Everest and the nearby Ama Dablam. The Khumbu Glacier is the world's highest glacier. It is disturbing that the ice is melting so rapidly at the earth's extremes, the highest mountain and the North Pole.

After leaving Arjun, Andrew films some beautiful time lapses of the changing light on the mountain, and I spend the rest of the day transferring footage back at our mess tent. I keep swinging back and forth on the Maoist issue. Bashista is saying one thing, Marshall another. My stomach clenches. I know it's indecision causing the anxiety. I am suspicious of

Bashista, certain that his smile hides manipulative intentions. I can feel the anger in my throat when I am around him now.

In the evening it's snowing again: time to go to my tent with water bottles. I have put three hard drives in the foot of my sleeping bag wrapped in big sweaters. I am craving some female energy; there's too much testosterone here. I have to get a grip on my anger—it will only make things harder for me.

Until we change our myths, we cannot change our minds.

UNDERSTANDING RISK

Morning takes my aggression away. It's bright out, even though the sun hasn't yet risen above the mountains. As I stretch I send out a small prayer for a good day guided by the force of a large, silent goddess. Again my back feels wretched from the hard protrusions through my mat. I am about half-way through my Base Camp adventure and thinking there must be a nicer way to put myself through hell.

My mom's brother Donald was in my dream, which took me to the small Acadian village where she was born: St.-Damien, New Brunswick. In the dream, I silently floated above the house where my grandmother used to live and saw an empty rocking chair slowly moving back and forth as if someone were sitting in it.

One foot in front of another. My climb isn't vertical at this point, but horizontal. I am looking for character reveals in my film subjects, and perhaps in myself.

There was a big snowfall last night. As I knock the snow off the roof of my tent, I can hear the tap and slide of others doing the same.

Andrew is hiking out with Bashista and Childon today to try and get some aerial views of Everest from nearby mountains Pumori and Kala Patthar. This will give me two days of alone time. The hike would have been good for me too, but I need to make sure one of us is at Base Camp with a camera at all times. When shooting a documentary, you never know when the proverbial shit will hit the fan and so I stay, watch, wait.

And I need a break from Bashista, our uninvited shadow—a fly I want to swat. I'm grateful he is going with Andrew, giving me a few days' respite. I have imaginary conversations with him in which I tell him to fuck off. Apparently my own darkness is creeping in.

Meagan leaves tomorrow for her summit push. She drops by for tea and to pick up a small portable camera so she can film herself as she makes her summit attempt. Conrad Anker is one of her heroes so she is giddy like a schoolgirl with a crush.

I look forward to a slow descent back into a living ecosystem twenty-one days from now.

DAY 19: MAY 8

Along with the usual bad back and rumbling gut, my night is filled with the sound of avalanches and some loud grumblings from beneath my tent. In the dark I smell burning juniper, so I unzip my tent just in time to see Meagan's silhouette and headlamp disappear up the Khumbu Icefall with her Sherpa guide. I am worried for all these climbers now as avalanches are happening with much more frequency.

In the morning, two ravens fly low over the prayer flags outside my tent. Framed by a white sky and white ice, the image is almost like a black and white photograph, except for the colour of the flags. Clouds cover the sun. No sunbeam warming the tent this morning makes it harder to get up. But the thought of coffee does it for me.

I walk over to join the Asian Trekking gang and find a sombre scene in the mess tent. Marshall, in a serious and sober tone, tells me a Russian climber has died. The man and his team had been climbing without a Sherpa. His teammates found him just outside his tent early this morning, dead of exposure. Apparently he died hanging onto a rope near Camp Four and remains frozen there. Marshall tells me the climber had a wife and three kids, and all I can think of as I hear these words is that his wife and kids don't know he is dead. Their lives are about to change forever and they don't know it yet, but I do.

For Marshall, the death brings up memories of past experiences of his time in the US army. He looks into my eyes from across the dining table and tells me he thinks in some ways Base Camp is a lot like Iraq.

"You have a group of high-risk people who join the military because they don't care about risk, and mountaineers climb mountains because they obviously don't care about the risks, or they don't understand them. It's one of those two things. And they are sort of surrounded by death and so there are certain defence mechanisms that crop up. They are the same in Iraq... When someone dies, it is not something you want to acknowledge. Even if they were your great friend you don't want to think about it too much. I see that here. When someone dies, a rumour goes around here very quickly. Some people make jokes, some people say it is too bad, but it is not dealt with in a normal way. Back home if you heard someone died you would have a totally different reaction, but that does not happen here." He shakes his head.

Around us people are laughing and joking. The show goes on. I remember hearing about a detached hand lying on the ground by the helicopter pad that remained there for weeks before it was tossed into the moraine and melting ice. As I share this with Marshall he tells me there are many more bodies and body parts showing up at Base Camp. As I'm thinking I need to film this, Bags walks into the tent with a blue plastic tube in her mouth that looks like an asthma inhaler. She is hauling off the thing. She has just walked back from the HRA tent and still plans on going back up the mountain. I think of Edvard Munch's *The Scream*.

Marshall has also had more news from Kathmandu. Everything there is shut down, and apparently tension is escalating. The people enforcing the boycott—a lot of disenfranchised young men—have become surly. As he speaks, Marshall doesn't look quite as comfortable with the situation as he did the other day. Again I feel the clenching in my belly.

At this point we hear a thunderous sound, like low-flying military jets roaring by, and run out to watch a big avalanche come down off the Icefall. It dawns on me that there actually could be an avalanche big enough to sweep through Base Camp. And again I am reminded that my tent is closest to the peaks towering beside Everest.

Like everyone here, I long for home. Everyone has a letter they keep rereading, or photos they keep looking at, something warm in this cold and brutal place, and something to look at to remember why you want to live if you get into trouble. I have a letter from Teresa I am supposed to read on my birthday here in a couple of weeks. I look at it every day.

I now feel that there is nothing noble in this quest. My childhood awe of the first summit has faded. Like everything else, it seems a selfish pursuit for fragile egos. Mine is one of them.

PICNIC AT A PLANE CRASH

DAY 20: MAY 9

Lots more avalanches early this morning. I wait in my tent for the sun to warm everything a bit before getting up and then I can hear an approaching helicopter. As I step outside, the helicopter is doing a circle over camp before landing. People shout and give the pilot the finger. The vibrations of the noisy engine can set off more avalanches, and most teams now have climbers somewhere on the mountain. To add to the cacophony, the Kazakhs blare the soundtrack from *Apocalypse Now*, and "Ride of the Valkyries" echoes off the ice and rock in the valley. I have to smile.

After breakfast, I wander over to the Kazakhstan mess tent to say hello I and discover the men are well into their beers and vodka—some more than others. Now the morning soundtrack makes sense. I assume they are drinking in memory of the Russian climber who died yesterday and their dead comrade from last year's expedition.

"Why do we do this?" Max asks as he pours me a vodka. "Sergei, who passed away one year ago, our friend, he had many children, and he knew what he was embarking upon. Right now, two days ago, another family lost their father. But this happens in life."

We all slam back our drinks in honour of their fallen comrades. Max tells me they plan to lower Sergei's body to Base Camp so they can give him a proper burial at the Everest graveyard near Lobuche.

I appreciate his loyalty to his dead friend and understand the strength that can be acquired testing oneself in nature. But as he speaks, running through my mind are the words of Mallory's son who once said he would rather have grown up with a living father than a dead legend.

DAY 21: MAY 10

At the Himalayan Rescue Association tent, Steve is talking to a new doctor named Eric about a patient they saw earlier this morning. Eric has been working at the HRA clinic at Pheriche for the past couple of months and is just here to help out for a few days. "We just sent out a forty-seven-year-old male anorexic. When the Sherpa found bowls of frozen rice tucked underneath the fly at Camp Two, he said, 'Hmmm, think we have a problem.' And then when he fell over it was like, 'Okay...'" Steve waves his arms like an umpire saying "You're out."

Inside the HRA tent, he answers a radio call about a climber they recently treated who suffered dangerous vertigo at Camp Two, couldn't walk a straight line and was vomiting. She wants to go up the mountain again, but Steve won't give her a medical release. He says the odds are she'd experience the symptoms again. Now she wants to go back to Kathmandu to get an MRI and CAT scan as part of a strategy to have a medical release to go back up the mountain.

"Problem is," he says, "these images are great—I would use them in Montana—but it won't give me information as to whether or not she is going to have symptoms of vertigo again going up, which would be a problem to the people guiding her."

I wonder aloud whether the trekking company has a hard time saying no to people who spend a lot of money to be here and if they look to the HRA for guidance.

"If she had the same symptoms of vertigo and couldn't walk straight, it puts not just her at risk, but the Sherpas and guides who would have to try and get her back down. And if they have to get a helicopter to get someone down from Camp Two, that can be very expensive. A slip and fall on Madison Avenue ain't a big deal. A slip and fall from the Lhotse Face because you forgot to clip in is a couple-thousand-metre fall. A small problem gets magnified on Everest. And it's a hard thing to grasp when you're waiting to get back up there."

A lot is happening beneath the thin veil of the surface at Base Camp, or in this case, beneath the thin plastic tents. I leave Steve and go back outside to talk to Eric again. His tent is just a few feet away from HRA. I ask him about his impressions so far.

"It's definitely a unique environment, definitely an interesting bunch of characters, a lot of very serious climbers with long climbing résumés, and then at the same time you have people who have very limited climbing experience, actually. Which for me is very interesting. I have never seen anything like this and I have climbed a fair bit in different places in the world."

I ask what he thinks about the woman who had vertigo and now wants to go back up the mountain.

"I think people spend a lot of time and a lot of money preparing to climb Everest, and I think it is a dream that is quite difficult to let go. It's part of the characteristic of the people who are drawn to this place, very driven. I heard a great quote from somebody: 'Only real egomaniacs want to climb 8,000-metre peaks.' And here you are at the biggest of the 8,000-metre peaks, so you take these people that are incredibly driven and incredibly focused who tend to be motivated and you start telling them that it's not safe, or your recommendation is that they don't climb the mountain, and it can be very, very difficult for them to process that and accept that. And I think that's the situation, even though from all the evidence we have it seems as though her climbing on this mountain could be a very dangerous situation not just for her but also for the guides and Sherpa."

This also applies to the anorexic climber, he says, pointing out that anorexia is control of the body and climbing Everest is control of the environment. "So I think it is a lot of the same personality traits, actually. It's not common here but it is not a big surprise to me."

I ask him if he has ever had to tell a person not to climb. And he said he had, although most already knew deep inside they shouldn't. "Actually, if anything I think some of them appreciate hearing that from a doctor. Because it is..." At this he pauses, smiles, and tilts his head. "Maybe it's a little harsh but I think it's true—it's an excuse. It allows them to go home with sort of the doctor's blessing saying that because of a medical problem they were unable to climb the mountain, not because of some failure on their part. So everyone I have to tell has accepted it quite well, unlike the lady you were discussing earlier."

On my way back to my mess tent, I scramble up the small scree hill between the HRA and Asian Trekking camp, where I find a middle-aged Nepali woman named Chunu. She is working as a government liaison for Asian Trekking and is one of seven Nepali women to have climbed Everest in 2008.

I ask what changes she has seen on the mountain.

"It is going down. It didn't used to look like this," she says, glancing around at the camp built on top of a dying glacier, the base of all the slopes around us just grey scree and moraine.

I ask about the bodies surfacing at Base Camp.

"Yes, because the ice is melting. Everybody knows about that, but everybody ignores it. I think we should stop climbing Everest, just for one, two, three years—just stop. Not going for a summit push, you know, just cleaning. Take out the dead bodies. It is difficult, you know, we are feeling so sad, because this is a god. It's big, top of the world, and it's melting. We need this fresh water also. This fresh water keeps many people alive."

It's true. One quarter of the world's population gets their drinking water from these Himalayan glaciers and snowmelt. I read that ice samples taken from the glacier last year have high levels of arsenic and cadmium, along with other heavy metals related to the pollution coming from the industrialization of China and India.

"There are many dead bodies, but here everybody couldn't care less, you know." Chunu points behind her and says, "Over there is a dead body—a dead hand and leg." Then, pointing to the other side: "Two dead bodies over there, also. But nobody cares."

I say, "Because it is bad for business."

"Yeah," Chunu agrees. "Because there is lots of money here, so why care about this?"

Of course the obvious reason to care is that these melting, contaminated glaciers filled with the dead are the source of the drinking water for everybody up here. We drink it, clean dishes with it, cook with it.

Arjun walks over and wishes Chunu and me a happy Mother's Day.

Chunu says thanks, but she doesn't have a child. Arjun asks me if I have a child, and I tell him no—if I did, it would be the second coming of Christ because I am married to a woman. Chunu gets a kick out of this, saying "All right" and cracking a big smile. I can see she really doesn't believe me so I say again, "It's true, a woman can marry another woman in Canada."

Chunu gives me a high-five. Arjun looks completely shocked—he has a nervous giddiness in his expression.

"How does Hinduism look at it?" I ask him.

"Hinduism is not liking it at all..." He trails off. "Don't put this in the film—this can be very controversial." At this, he walks away.

Currently in India homosexual acts of love will get you ten years in jail. I didn't come here to wave a flag, but in joking about it I did just that. After Arjun walks away I turn back to Chunu and tell her I want to film the dead bodies emerging through the ice at Base Camp. I ask if she knows where they are. She thinks it is a good idea but says she can't take me there. I can see the discussion makes her nervous.

After talking to Chunu I think about how we are all camping on a burial ground of human remains. No wonder this places feels weird. It's like having a picnic on top of a plane crash, with dismembered body parts strewn about.

I hike back for lunch and find Andrew and the boys are back. The hike went well. Andrew says he got some nice shots of Everest from the top of Kala Patthar. Bashista is concerned about getting us on a plane out of Lukla. He has a map on the table suggesting the hiking route we should take back. Bit early to fret about that, I think. If he wants to leave, I tell him, please go. But he won't leave until we do. Kathmandu is still politically unstable. He tells me that seven soldiers from the communist league showed up at Base Camp looking to collect some forced donations. In Canada we call that extortion.

After Andrew leaves the mess tent Bashista suggests I give him some money to give to them. I explain to him that the only money I have left is tip money for the crew. If he wants to donate their tips to the Maoists, I will gladly hand that over to him to do so. This shuts Bashista right up.

After twenty days the melting and shifting glacier has already profoundly reshaped the environment. It is time to rebuild the platform under my tent, now sitting four feet higher than the ground around it so I have a riverfront suite.

Every morning I cross the date off, like those advent calendars with little windows—a chocolate a day until Christmas. The countdown gives me a sense of progress and builds excitement. Twenty-four days to go before I kiss the ground in Canada.

I am spending more and more time in my tent. Both Andrew and I are showing signs of fatigue. And fatigue wears down tolerance.

THE DARKNESS AND
THE LIGHT

I am no longer fazed when I wake to yet another avalanche on the slope to my left. It's still windy, but the sun is rising in blue skies today, and Miloh is singing in the mess tent. With two weeks to go, there is mounting excitement for most climbers as they approach their final push for the summit.

A Canadian woman from Newfoundland reached the peak two days ago but had difficulty getting down. She left Base Camp right away for lower altitudes. It's a strange feeling knowing that it's quite possible another climber will die here in the next two weeks. I hope I am wrong, but the risk factors, coupled with the number of people going up, make it seem inevitable.

Meagan is just back from Camp Three, white zinc all over her nose and a red, sunburnt face. She says she had some sleep apnea on this rotation. She wants to try to climb Lhotse without oxygen, so hasn't used oxygen on her acclimatization hikes, which made sleeping at Camp Three a bit of a struggle. She tells me there were clear skies but strong winds at Camp Three, with some gusts of over 80 kilometres an hour. Her team had weather reports, but as usual they were all wrong.

Camp Three, Meagan explains, is on a steep cliff, so you really only have about 2.5 metres around the walls of your tent to move around safely. The winds really picked up during the night she spent there, and in the morning her team awoke to find their tents were buried in snow. Coming down from Camp Three the winds were "crazy," she adds, saying that the only other place she experienced that was Antarctica.

Meagan is still pumped with the adrenalin of this last rotation. I can see she climbs mountains not because she isn't afraid, but to challenge her fears and in doing so to feel stronger and more competent. You never feel as alive as you do after coming close to death, she tells me.

Arjun walks over and decides to share some bowel stories. I would say it is his age—guys at sixteen love fart jokes—but in fairness, at Base Camp everyone talks about their bowels. Arjun says every time he starts trekking he has to go, so he is going to carry a rest stop bag to the top.

Today is my little sister's forty-first birthday, so I walk over to the Asian Trekking puja and send her a telepathic message. There's crazy energy in the air. Andrew is lying down in his tent with hot and cold compresses, having woken up with a bad shoulder. Miloh's assistant has dropped a basket of rocks on his hand and nearly severed a finger, and Marshall and Arjun are looking for Brad Pitt. Rumours have been circulating for weeks that he is here. Marshall posted the rumour on his blog and now TMZ is reporting that he is here. Marshall isn't sure if it is just a feedback loop or if it's really true. I grab a camera and follow them on their quest.

I find it funny. Before leaving Vancouver I would refer to Mt. Everest as the Brad Pitt of mountains because it is a good-looking celebrity that can fetch a price of a hundred thousand dollars for the privilege of trying to climb to the top. Now here I am, looking for the guy himself. We head toward the helicopter landing pad near the entrance to Base Camp. It is the first time I have walked to the other side of camp since arriving. It takes about forty-five minutes. Now that I have committed to our characters our days are tethered to the fifteen-minute radius around our camp, so I'm glad to be stepping outside that and hiking with the boys. Marshall has heard that Pitt's team is set up just outside the outer edge of the tents, staying low-key with a couple of porters. We approach three green medium-sized tents that fit the description and find a couple of Korean climbers who just smile and say, "No Brad Pitt, ha ha ha ha!"

After a few laughs ourselves we push on toward the landing pad as we can hear a helicopter coming into camp. I'm hoping to get some close-ups of it landing. The roar is deafening. The landing is quick. As soon as it touches down, supplies come off, a sick woman and a lot of bags get thrown on and off it goes. You can never count on good weather lasting long when you're high up in the Himalayas.

On our way back to camp, we stop by the HRA tent, where I am shocked to see a young Sherpa man, Miloh's assistant, standing there with a half-amputated finger waiting his turn. Inside the tent there's an American family of trekkers, here for a few hours, who want to buy T-shirts from the HRA. Sometimes it is an embarrassment to be white. This is one of those moments. The young injured man speaks no English so I gesture for him to follow me into the tent, and I film him walking in with his hand covered in blood, which expedites the departure of the rude tourists. I almost faint at one point myself—the telephoto-lens close-up of the finger being sewn back on is a little too much detail for me.

After leaving the HRA tent, I reconnect with Marshall and Arjun at the Asian Trekking camp. They both offer to come with me to where one of the dead bodies is coming out of the ice just outside our camp. Rumour has it there are four more bodies surfacing in the melting ice at Base Camp. I find it disconcerting that nothing is being done to remove them.

It is eerie as we approach the mound of ice the body is entombed in. All we can see from the surface is a hand, still reaching up, frozen in its final act. As we get closer, the smell of death hits us. What was frozen for years is now rotting by day and refreezing every night. A handful of people at this camp are bearing witness to the recovery of someone who was lost. I feel guilty for seeing the art in the image: the hand framed by the top of a mountain and a string of prayer flags. I am struck by the colour, the composition. I frame the image and click several shots under the shadowed gaze of several pairs of disdainful eyes peering from tent doorways. When I look closer I realize the guy making me feel most guilty is a Nepali filmmaker, who I later learn has already filmed the same scene. Apparently a photo of this hand was also taken by a climber and filed to

National Geographic. I continue to film as Marshall places a blue tarp over the hand. All three of us are quiet and sombre after seeing the dead man. I say a quiet prayer, walk back to our office tent and tell Andrew I have just shot our film poster. He is up and his shoulder is feeling a bit better.

During lunch in the dining tent, Bashista tells us there is going to be a meeting of the Sagarmartha Pollution Control Committee (SPCC) to decide what to do with all the bodies emerging from the ice. We pack up all the gear. Childon carries Andrew's camera, Andrew carries the tripod, I carry the sound gear and Bashista carries a clipboard, and we all hike over to the SPCC tent. SPCC's mission is to free the Khumbu region of pollution, but so far I haven't gotten a good vibe from these guys. They are supposed to be stewards of the environment but I have yet to see any one of them pick up any garbage. They walk around camp in an arrogant and imposing way, like shady union bosses.

I think they are Maoists. I understand the seduction of Maoism for the poor working class of Nepal. It just sounds so damn good: rising up of the workers, equality for all, putting an end to the class system... *blah, blah, blah.* I was seduced by those ideas myself as a young adult but as I have gotten older I have come to believe strongly in the rights of the individual, not just the collective.

About fifty people have gathered for the meeting. Apa, Dawa, Bashista, Childon and Chunu are among them. What I do not know at the time, and won't know until much later, is that as I sit there filming the meeting (in Nepali), thinking they're discussing what to do with the dead bodies, they are also discussing whether or not to censor my film because I just photographed one of those bodies.

After the meeting Bashista tells me that Chunu, the only woman at the meeting, was "a bad lady." He says that she is the one who told members of the SPCC I had filmed the dead body. Naturally my blood boils, but without speaking the language I really don't know who said what. I feel vulnerable. All our work is on hard drives. If somebody wanted to stop us from making this film, all they would have to do is steal the hard drives or pick them up and throw them down on some rock and poof! All the footage would disappear. How do you lock a tent? Any pocketknife can rip through a wall in seconds. Now I am paranoid at Base Camp. And the darkness creeps in closer.

DAY 23: MAY 12

They will be removing bodies from the icefield for the next three days. Andrew and I start the day in our office tent, prepping our cameras and discussing what approach we should take to film one of the bodies being chipped out of the ice. Bashista says we shouldn't do it at all, telling us that it would be bad to do so and might invoke violent behaviour. Andrew and I have decided to do it anyway. We will film with a long lens and position ourselves a short distance from the action.

Arjun finds me as I'm drinking my morning tea to tell me that Chunu did not slam me at the meeting—if that's true, Bashista is lying. When I question him, Bashista maintains he is telling the truth, but won't sit in a tent with Chunu and me to clear the air. So he's lying. I could force the issue, and I want to, but I know it would just make matters worse. And after the Maoist thing, why did I even doubt that he is the liar? We hike to our position and set up equipment, and all along the way, Bashista warns me that people will break our camera. I reply that they might encounter some resistance from me and we carry on.

A few dozen people have gathered around the men digging out the corpse. Every one of them has a consumer camera, and they are all clicking away. The Nepali filmmaker even puts his camera inches from where the pick strikes the ice to dig out the bones. We are the only ones to stand back respectfully. I don't mind if there is a rule or a custom I am asked to respect if the rule applies to everybody. But clearly that's not the case here. Some guy in the crowd gives Andrew and me the finger and tells us to "shut off the fucking camera."

Andrew asks what to do, and I tell him to keep filming. I can see the issue is not respect for the dead. I think these guys don't want me to show this aspect of Everest in my film because it might be bad for business. Hard to charge $100,000 for someone to come and camp in a place full of bodies and garbage. They are motivated by their self-interest.

I am too. And I realize it's bringing out anger, rebellion and a fuck-you attitude in all of us. A shadow closes in again. I can feel the potential for violence in and around me. If someone rips into me or tries to damage my camera I'm primed to rip back.

But no one interferes, and we film for an hour as the remains are slowly chipped out of the ice with ice picks. The whole of what used to be a person comes out in parts. Bleached bones, bits of clothing, strands of hair, all pieces placed into a bag.

After the intense morning, Andrew decides to take my still camera and film Base Camp pickup shots: clips of the various flags and wide shots of the camp. I go to my tent to reflect. I feel myself shutting down, my actions coming from the hard place in my heart. I feel defensive, aggressive and at the same time terribly sad. A short while later Andrew appears to tell me he has had a mishap with the camera. He had it mounted to the tripod and a strong wind blew it over and smashed it. I will be paying off an $11,000 lease for the next three years for a piece of broken equipment.

Every journey has a cracking point and this is mine. I know I have to keep it together and stay focused, but I am feeling overwhelmed. I knew there would be tough moments here. I expected and have endured many physical ones, but today's are emotional. The wind is howling, I have been told to fuck off. I feel the social conventions eroding, the untamed coming to the surface. And for the first time at Base Camp, I cry.

Buddhism is about understanding the truth of the mind and the nature of existence. Buddhism, which for 2,500 years has cultivated direct observation of the mind, is structured upon four noble truths, the first of which is that all life is suffering. Evil is a natural part of the order of things and a consequence of human actions. The dark is as natural as the light.

I feel alone. Judgment is a cold wind. When I close my eyes I see the frozen hand, reaching up. I can taste the smell of rotting flesh in my throat.

I stay in my tent for the rest of the day and night. At dinnertime Miloh brings garlic soup and a pappadum to my tent. Andrew comes by with more, and even Bashista brings me fruit and says he is sorry my camera broke. I feel grateful for the kindness.

The Everest graveyard at 4840 metres (15,479 feet). In the foreground a few of the dozens of rock cairns memorializing some of those who have died on Everest.

Thousands of porters walk the 100 kilometre trail to Everest Base Camp every April and May. The average porter carries 20-25 kilos.

Accommodations along the trail were at tea lodges like this one, Benkar Lodge, between Lukla and Namche.

The arch of the Tengboche Monastery.

Yaks are central to Sherpa culture. They provide milk for cheese, fur for clothing and can handle high-altitudes for transporting goods to Base Camp.

Elderly Sherpa woman at a monastery above Thame.

For most of the year strong jet stream winds pummel the summit of Everest making summit attempts impossible. When the Monsoon season begins in May the jet stream normally shifts to the north of Everest creating a weather window. Climbers watch for no winds, and blue skies.

As the Khumbu glacier melts, dead bodies and body parts surface at Base Camp. These climbers died years ago higher up the mountain but the glacier has slowly dragged them down and climate change is bringing them to the surface.

Every April and May Base Camp at Everest becomes a temporary town of over 1000 people from around the world, but no one is in charge. It is a town without a sheriff.

The drinking water at Base Camp comes from streams of the melting Khumbu glacier.

Canadian climber Meagan McGrath sitting on the peak of Lhotse, the fourth highest mountain in the world.

Arjun Vajpai, 16 years old, at Base Camp attempting to be the youngest Indian to climb Everest.

Colombian climber Nelson Carvajal wants to climb Everest to show that disability is just a state of mind. Photo by Carolina Ahumada Cala.

This is the view of Everest a few hours before reaching Base Camp. You can't see the peak of Everest from Base Camp.

At Base Camp working for the Nepalese Government, Bashista Adhikari. His job was to stay with the film crew. It was a love/hate relationship.

Our camp: My tent is on the left, and Andrew's is on the right.

Camp 1 Mt. Everest. Photo by Juan Pablo.

This tent is perched on a small ledge at Camp 3 and is looking down the steep climb up from Camp 2 and beyond. Photo by Arjun Vajpai.

Andrew Coppin shooting some footage. Andrew was the Director of Photography on my documentary film, *40 Days at Base Camp*.

SURFACING

DAY 24: MAY 13

Grace. Courage. Strength.

The nights bring out fear. In the deep darkness, I hear someone walking around my tent, see a flashlight bouncing around my exterior walls. I grab my Swiss army knife and sit in a state of high alert. I am still really scared that our footage will be stolen. I have locked it up in a duffel bag in our kitchen tent, but a sharp knife could cut through that, and everybody carries one of those.

It's terrifying to feel frail in a harsh environment. I'm no better than any ego on this mountain. I'm filming human remains because it's part of the story but also because it will help sell mine. But being called out by men who set their cameras even closer to the image is sexism or prejudice. Whatever you want to call it, it's unfair. I'll own my shit but I'm not taking theirs.

Grace. Courage. Strength. My mantra. Hold it together, Dee.

The winds gust to 80 kilometres an hour.

10 A.M.

The Canadian men were supposed to leave today but after a weather update, they think the winds will be too strong on the summit, so they have decided to hold off for the May 21 window. They plan to stay acclimatized by doing day hikes and staying at Base Camp instead of going to Camp Two to wait. They are under some time pressure. This morning's weather report said that the monsoon season is active now. Typically the monsoon starts over the Bay of Bengal in the south and moves toward Everest. When the monsoon gets going, it basically shuts the mountain down.

Rob is missing his kids and breaks down when we ask him to read one of his emails. He has three kids. The mountains took their toll on the relationship he has with their mother. He is now in a new relationship with a woman who is also involved in raising awareness about intestinal issues, and he works hard at a friendship with his ex for the sake of their girls.

Rob jokes that patience is a virtue, knowing now they will wait another week. "You get what you get, but I would rather wait on decent weather than rush and get caught in something that is going to be nasty. It's the mountains—you don't always get what you want but it's worth the wait."

Everyone says it is warmer up here than it was last year, which is why there is more concern over the icefield. Consensus says that it is more volatile and dangerous than usual. "The conservative forecast," Guide John explains, "calls for high winds over Everest, and it is going to split off in a few days, a little lower but still above 50 kilometres per hour. Anything above that is really raising a chance of frostbite on the mountain. Keeping warm is the big issue. It may be nice weather but the winds are still going to be high.

"Right now Base Camp is split. Ten to fifteen teams are now at Camp Two waiting for the summit bid. There are lots of rumours flying around for the sixteenth and seventeenth. [There are] many different forecasts that we have been looking at, and there are many different opinions, as you know how forecasts go. We are choosing to take the more conservative role. Two out of three forecasts say it is going to be high winds. That's good enough for me; we are going to wait a little later."

We need fuel for our generator in order to recharge the large batteries for the Panasonic 500, and the Canadians kindly offer some to us for free. Childon is getting a 5-litre tank filled with the help of their Sherpa team. I am grateful for their kindness. The Koreans are selling fuel for six hundred rupees a litre. In Kathmandu the price is eighty rupees. As the Sherpa pours it out for us, we get a good whiff of the fumes. Andrew says it reminds him of home because that is what our society is built on.

THE COLOMBIANS

Standing with the Icefall behind him, Juan Pablo tells us the Colombian team is leaving for their summit push today. The sky is blue, there is a wind and it's already 11 a.m.

Today they will go to Camp Two. Tomorrow they will take a rest day and check the weather again. Right now the forecast is not the best, but Juan Pablo says the big companies like Russell Brice's Himalyan Eperience, which has forty clients, are waiting for a better window after May 20, which is why Juan Pablo wants to take the risk now to avoid the traffic jam. They hope to push from Camp Four on the night of the sixteenth to reach the summit the morning of the seventeenth. If it doesn't work, they will come back and do it again May 20–25 with the traffic jam.

Andrew asks Juan how he feels about going into the Icefall at this time of day. These are all professional climbers but the other pros have hit the glacier before 4 a.m. The Colombians have a more laid-back attitude, preferring to enjoy a morning coffee.

"I would say the Icefall is dangerous anytime, I mean twenty-four hours," Juan replies, telling us that the day before they were thinking of going early but there was a big avalanche at 5 a.m. that was very close to people already in the Icefall. "Sometimes at night you can hear more avalanches than in the day. But of course we understand midday can be more dangerous because it is warming. But we know it is never safe in the mountains."

MEAGAN

After lunch I find Meagan behind the mess tent doing laundry. She squats between two large steel bowls perched on some rocks, one filled with clear hot water and the other filled with grey water. She uses a small cereal bowl to scoop some clean hot water and pours it over a dirty sock and some soap in another small bowl. After washing the sock, she pours the dirty water into the grey water bowl and puts the clean sock with some others on a rock.

Meagan is wearing a white surgical mask. She picked up a bit of a cough coming down from Camp Three, she says, but seems confident she will get better. She looks strong.

Three teams on the mountain are trying to summit. One weather report indicates a window May 15. A second report calls for a window May 23. Meagan and Apa's group is going for the latter. After the summit, she'll go right back down to Camp Two that day and back to Base Camp the next morning. Meagan says if she summits May 23, she will be back at Base Camp on May 25 and will try to leave by May 27. I had no idea they descended from the summit so quickly. What goes up comes down much quicker here in the Himalayas.

Ideally the weather window would be a little longer, but who knows? she says. The weather reports have been really bad this year. It's hard to trust them. Having just come down, she wants some time to recover, do her laundry and get strong for the summit push.

Because Meagan is trying to climb Lhotse without oxygen, she needs the temperatures to be just right. When you are not using oxygen, blood circulation is not as good so you are more prone to frostbite.

As more socks get washed, our discussion turns to Base Camp. She asks me how I am doing and I can tell she has heard something about my tearfest. Nothing happens in private here. But I know if I talk about crying yesterday, I just might start again, so I bury it beneath a smile. Meagan says, "This place tests you, whether you are here to make a film or climb a mountain. It's like, are you here to do what you want to do or are you going to get caught up in someone else's drama? It's up to you."

I silently nod my head in agreement as I film her doing her laundry. I knew Base Camp would test me, I knew it was going to be hard, but I perceived the difficulties as external challenges. What sideswiped me was all the internal reflection. Some days it feels more like a pilgrimage than a film shoot.

"Fuck 'em," Meagan says. "You have something to do here, just do it. There are people who like you—hang out with them. That's it. That's life, eh? People talk about other people all the time, that is the way it is."

"Weird place, Meagan," I say.

"I know, not necessarily good, just its own little place. Accept it for what it is… Even in terms of the mountaineering world, it is not a common base camp environment. You have to take it for what it is. If you don't, you might get sensitive. It might hurt you. Just do what you are here to do, just do it. Fuck everyone else. Not in a bad way, just don't get caught up in their drama and let it hurt you. Help other people, be concerned about other people, but don't get so entwined that you're losing sight of your goal."

As I hike back to our dining tent I film some close-ups of the melting ice. What started as a drip weeks ago is now flowing like a tap, and the small tributaries have merged into a shallow but wide river flowing past our camp. I think, for centuries in human literature the mountain has been a place where people come for reflection. As the ice melts and reveals the dead and the garbage, so too does the time here reveal what is beneath the surface of myself and those around me. The shit is coming to the surface.

Crying was painful and made me feel vulnerable, but it opened the hearts of those around me. As Bashista says, when we see good, there is good everywhere. When we see bad, there is bad everywhere.

ENDURANCE TESTS

DAY 25: MAY 14

I wake in the night, thinking I am having a heart attack or stroke—heart beating like crazy, feet and hands instantly sweating, anxiety kicking in. I try to slow my breathing down with deep breaths, strip off my coat, undo my bra strap and in a small panic find a vial of Bach Flower Rescue Remedy for calming the mind and body. Usually I would just put a few drops under my tongue but I drink the entire bottle.

I think I have what Chinese medicine calls liver wind: my liver and gallbladder are not happy. A lot of the food here is fried; maybe that's my problem. I'm going to knock off fried food and coffee. It takes a while but the Rescue Remedy kicks in. I start to feel calmer and my heart slows down to a fast walk from a sprint.

I'm supposed to leave in just under two weeks. Of course now the summit thing is an albatross. Despite all the rope, satellite phones and Internet, nature has the final say. I imagine crazy tension if an early monsoon steals the show. I'm feeling burnt out. I gird myself for another day: filming for a few hours, then four hours transferring footage and backing it up. It's an endurance test. The shortness of breath stays with me all day. This goes against the logic of acclimatization—it should be easier to breathe now, not harder. Makes me wonder if last night's episode was a small heart attack rather than anxiety.

After I get up I go up the small hill to the Asian Trekking camp. Arjun and Meagan are hanging out with Marshall in the communications tent, sitting there with their big down coats on. This is the waiting game. Today there is talk around camp that some people are waiting for a weather window on May 27, during which time the monsoon will push the jet stream out of the way, keeping wind off the peak for a few days. Long-term forecasts are calling for it to be good May 20–27.

Meagan is glad, as a longer weather window means not everybody will be running up the mountain on the same day. Apparently forty people are on the mountain now, going for a summit push. Meagan says she was freezing all night. "I have an old MEC sleeping bag. It was rated for minus ten degrees, but it has been washed too many times so I think it is a plus five now." She laughs. Meagan is an aerospace engineer for the Canadian Air Force. She has been with the Canadian Forces for almost twenty years. She jokes that she is getting ready to retire, which she can do in 2015. She has some sponsors for her climbing but not enough to survive on. She has no interest in starting her own expedition company or in getting paid to take other people up the mountain. She intends to apply to go to Afghanistan when she gets back in a few months. Right now she works an office job, on the phone, writing emails, taking meetings and solving problems.

The conversation turns to ski jumping and the Olympics of three months ago. The female ski jumpers wanted to be able to compete like the men could, but they were once again denied the chance. Meagan and Marshall are trying to figure out what logical reason could possibly exist that would rationalize the IOC's decision not to let the women compete. "I assume it has something to do with breasts," says Marshall.

"It has fuck all to do with boobs," replies Meagan. "That's stupid."

"I am not saying I agree with it," says Marshall. "I am saying if you ask the IOC guy why women ski jumpers weren't being allowed in, I bet you five bucks he would say something to do with boobs."

Meagan's not buying it. "Because he has nothing else to base it on, because he is full of crap. That's like saying men shouldn't play basketball because their penises get in the way when they jump."

Everybody laughs and Marshall stands up, saying he has to go give Apa a hand dealing with some cheap sponsors. "Some people try to send things up with Apa without paying," he explains. "This is his livelihood and every item that you have to take up makes it more dangerous." Marshall tells us that Apa has a friend named Jerry who usually handles all this stuff for him, "but Jerry is not here. I am here. I don't do this kind of stuff so it's kind of stressing me out."

"Just look mean and stroke your beard," I tell him.

Marshall does a demonstration, but it doesn't look convincing. He is a mild-mannered, calm and gentle man. I ask him if Apa gets bothered with requests like that often.

"Yeah, lots of people want him to carry banners, toys, it's crazy," he says, and he leaves on his mission.

After a lunch of garlic soup and crackers I head over to check up on Carolina at the Colombian tent. She is listening to some music from the coast of Colombia, traditional rhythms fused with modern rhythms. Her team is all on the mountain, and she is checking in with weather reports. The wind is now predicted to be 16 to 32 kilometres per hour instead of 32 to 48 kilometres per hour, so she is happy about that. They get their weather reports from Belgium, a company called Weather4Expeditions run by a guy named Mark. The forecasts are good but Carolina says after ninety-six hours he can't know for sure. So she is somewhat skeptical of the bulk of people at Base Camp believing in long-range forecasts calling for good weather May 20–27. She thinks that assumption is based on what has happened in previous years.

"Our Sirdar says, 'I don't trust weather reports, this is the mountains, anything can happen. See and wait, and if you see it is good you go up.'" She laughs. "You can have all these weather reports and information but in the end"—she touches her coat where her heart is—"it is about a feeling and a connection to nature, I think. Instinct. Mark says it is a very tight window. Juan Pablo says if we are fast, if we don't find traffic jams on the fixed lines, he thinks they can make it. They are in Camp Two right now because at Camp Three there is too much wind. And in Camp Two they are comfortable. They have a dining tent and a cook, and Camp Two is protected from the wind by some rocks."

Carolina explains that because the winds are supposed to pick up again, if they do summit they will have to come down very fast. They are on target to push for a summit on the sixteenth.

TRASH FOR CASH

DAY 26: MAY 15

Dawa Steven has arrived at Base Camp to be there for his clients' push for the summit. He assures me the Maoists are not a problem and Kathmandu is calming down. Andrew and I set up an interview right on the Khumbu Glacier with prayer flags hanging behind him.

"Back in my father's time there were only a handful of companies doing this," he tells us as he points around at all the other expedition tents. "To be frank, my father was an innovator in this field. He was the biggest operator back in the 1990s and he did some amazing things. But there were only five companies that could seriously outfit an expedition, and of those we are one of the few that have lasted nearly three decades. For me and my family, it is not just about climbing; it is about the Sherpas, because we ourselves are Sherpas. We are giving employment to local people and we are helping the local economy, so that is also a big bonus for us. It's our lifestyle more than our job."

Like every Sherpa I have spoken to, Dawa is concerned about climate change. Sherpas make their living from the mountains. As he says, "The mountains, as you can see with your own eyes, are literally melting. This makes it more and more dangerous, not just for mountaineers who are subject to the threats of avalanches and rock falls and serac collapses, but also to local people, who depend on the glaciers for water. And [there is] also the threat that big glaciers pose when they become big lakes that burst and come down and flood the whole valley and can wash away infrastructure, houses, farms and even people and livestock."

When he climbed Everest in 2008, Dawa carried a banner that said,

"Save the Himalayas," intended to bring attention to climate change on Everest. I ask him about the dead bodies popping up at Base Camp as a result of the ice melting. Might not that also bring some attention to climate change?

"In the past three or four years we have been noticing that more and more bodies are showing up out of the glacier. Many of them are mountaineers who died up in the Icefall or higher up in the Western Cwm, and whether they died in the 1960s or just recently, the glacier swallows them up, and as the glacier moves down towards Base Camp the bodies start popping up again. And part of the reason why the bodies start popping up is because the ice melts. Maybe another reason we are seeing dead bodies is because of the cleanup as well. The Sherpas and porters are searching the Icefall and Base Camp for garbage and in doing so are finding dead bodies. Definitely we are noticing that the ice is melting quite dramatically, and a lot of old stuff is coming out including dead bodies. For us climbers, it is really quite demotivating to see a dead body, especially one that has not had a proper burial. One that looks like it is in a state of anguish."

With over 250 dead bodies still on the mountain, this problem is going to be an ongoing one. The dying glacier revealing the dead bodies is a siren call about climate change for me. But I can see why Dawa wants a softer way of communicating the concerns. This is his business.

Dawa points out that handling dead bodies, especially unidentified ones, is complicated. "It's not just like garbage. You can't just take it away and dump it somewhere. It is a human being."

Even so, as I witnessed earlier, the bones of the dead were in fact put into the same white bags used for collecting garbage. Strange dichotomy of the pujas and prayer flags on one hand, and the dead bodies and body parts on the other.

"It's not only the liaison officers and the Ministry of Tourism that are involved, but also the Home Ministry and the police who have to be involved, and a death certificate has to be written," Dawa explains. "This year, we knew where all the dead bodies were but took more than a month until we were all ready and before we were all motivated enough to say, forget the paperwork, forget the official procedure because that's not practical at this altitude in Base Camp where even police say they can't make it up here.

"So we had to get as many members of Nepali civil society [as possible] together and we wrote out an entire paper as witnesses saying we had found these dead bodies and something had to be done, and if anybody is going to have any issues about this then they were going to have to talk to all of us, and forty-one people signed this paper. After that we identified three different bodies in the Icefall and split into three teams, and within one morning we gathered all the dead bodies in the glacier and we buried them. In fact, the body my team found in the glacier was a whole body and some Sherpas were able to identify the man who actually died in 2006, and the family was contacted and the body was shipped back to his village, portered back to his village, and he had a proper Buddhist burial with his family there, which means his soul is now at peace."

Somehow I don't think the body we filmed being chipped out of the ice is going to have a restful soul.

As Dawa talks I can't help but think that my filming of the dead body has contributed to their motivation. For the time I've been here it seems they've avoided the fact that dead bodies were popping up. I haven't noticed any candlelight vigils, moments of silence, lamas or reverence. And I've been told that the severed human hand that lay on the rocks by the helicopter pad was eventually just picked up and tossed out of view.

As dark as this is, Dawa's generation brings a new sensibility to Base Camp. "When I came here in 2007, everywhere you could see tin cans, bones, discarded gas bottles, all sorts of garbage because there was no incentive for new expeditions to clean up the garbage of old expeditions. During the monsoon when the glacier melts, more old garbage comes out, so garbage we couldn't see last year we can see this year, and I'm sure there will be more old garbage coming out in the future as more ice melts."

A few years ago Dawa recognized an opportunity when he thought about the rotations that people do up the mountain and started a program called "Trash for Cash." When the Sherpas go up they bring loads with them, and then they come back empty-handed. So Dawa approached all the Sherpas and other climbing companies and told them he would pay them by the kilo to pick up garbage on the mountain. In 2008 almost 1,000 kilos were collected, and in 2009 almost 6,000 kilos were collected. So far this year they are at 5,000 kilos.

DOMESTIC BLISS

DAY 27: MAY 16

The skies are sunny, and it is so warm in my tent. In just a few days I will spend my birthday on Everest for the second time. It could also be a summit day for some of my characters. It's great to be so close to packing up. I wake up and tick the day's date off a calendar, in excitement not for a day to come, but for one more day behind me.

In my dreams last night I was longboarding on a motorized board at a large airport, about to go on a trip with no luggage. An estranged acquaintance named Egan was leading me to my folks, where a reporter for the *Financial Post* took my photo. My dogs were in a room somewhere and I was desperately looking for Teresa. She was gone.

My tent is now four feet up from the walking surface. Soon I may need a ladder to get into it. I put on my last clean pair of long johns, a clean pair of socks and a clean shirt. I have no more clean pants. At breakfast I find Bashista has shaved his beard and Miloh has shaved his head. Andrew is doing some handwashing of laundry. I'm the least domesticated person in my crew.

I'm told there is another Maoist uprising in Kathmandu. I go to Asian Trekking's camp. Those who are waiting to summit are finding it hard to be patient. The training, the prep and the non-stop *go, go, go* are followed by a big pause while they wait for the right moment. Meagan and Dawa are standing outside drinking tea, discussing the fact that the steeper parts of Lhotse are currently not roped. The trick for Meagan will be making those high-altitude decisions with no oxygen, so she is trying to problem-solve possible scenarios down here while she is waiting. The

Lhotse Face is 2 kilometres of vertical ice. Even on oxygen people have suffered vertigo coming down the face.

I ask whether she will be bringing some oxygen up so she has it in case she needs it.

"We have emergency oxygen," Meagan says. "If something isn't going cool, I can put it on and come back down. But I'm not using it just for clarity, because that is the whole point of a no-oxygen ascent. If I do that, I might as well use oxygen the whole way."

Meagan's decision not to use oxygen is a personal one. She wants to test herself, to see how she does above 8,000 metres without it. It's something that she has seen done by climbers she respects.

"It is something to aspire to," she says. "You do it step by step. I have a safety bottle, all the backup systems I can without me using oxygen directly, and yes, it is because people I know who climb really well and people who I admire tried it without oxygen. I am not saying I am like them, but you have to start somewhere and take it step by step, and you don't know if you don't try. Right now, I am a bit worried about coming down, so I'm trying to change my thinking. I can't be unsure."

At this point Arjun walks over and we wander over to the Bad Finns. They have some Base Camp services, a cook and one Sherpa for one of them who is going to climb Everest. The other two are going to try to climb Lhotse independently. They have set up their own camps and know if they get in trouble they can't count on support unless they are willing to pay for it. That's business, that's Base Camp. They admit to shooting rocks at my tent with a slingshot.

"Bastards," I jokingly tell them, and I stumble over the growing river and up a small hill of scree back over to the Colombian team where I find Carolina coughing in her communication tent. She looks stressed. She asks me about my day, and I tell her about my interview with Dawa about garbage. She said she knows the mountains are sacred for the Sherpas, but she saw porters and Sherpas throwing garbage on the trail hiking in.

"Last time I was walking with my Sirdar, I saw a paper on the ground so I bent down and picked it up, and he said, 'Oh, what are you doing?' I said,

'I want to put this in the garbage can.' And he said, 'Oh no, leave it here, give it to me.' And he put it under a rock. It is a matter of education, I think."

Carolina has an ecotourism company in Colombia and is building awareness about how to be more ecologically sound in tourism. She encourages reusable water bottles, gives her clients canvas bags to use instead of plastic, and has seen first-hand that some people are open to change, others not. She says she also realizes through her company how disconnected from nature people have become. She has had educated clients from cities who don't know that pineapples grow on trees.

Some members of the Colombian team are on their way to Camp Four; they will push for the summit tonight at 7 p.m. Carolina will need to be in constant radio contact at that point but so far has had no luck making contact from her camp, so she will have to hike to another tent. One of the team, Antonio, has turned around from Camp Three because he lost feeling in half his body.

She is nervous because according to an updated weather report, they will have to leave the summit more quickly than they thought. But she cannot reach them to let them know.

I tell Carolina I will come and see her later tonight—partly as a filmmaker following my story, but also partly as a friend who wants to be with her should something go wrong on the mountain. I head back over to my mess tent to charge batteries and download P2 cards. With summit attempts now approaching I need to be ready at all times.

En route I bump into Mumta, a forty-year-old schoolteacher from India. She's staring at the sunny slopes of the Icefall. "That is my dream," she beams as she points to the mountain. "You want to do something for a long time, and you get it and this time I hug the mountain." And she laughs. "'Cause I love mountains, so it's a great moment at the top, maybe, if the mountain allows me."

"What's your next dream?" I ask.

"After this I climb K2," she says. "More dangerous peak."

I ask her why she likes danger, and whether she has been like that since she was a child.

"No," she says. "As a child, so scared of all dangers, but now this time, I am not." Again she laughs. "I take risks. You know you have scary points, but there is safety in being scared, so fear is a little bit good. It is necessary."

As I continue on my way to my camp I see Dawa Steven sitting by his tent. A day of no wind at Base Camp feels like summer. I tell him the Colombians are heading up for a summit push tonight.

"What mask are they using? Are they using the Russian mask or the British mask?"

I ask him what the difference is.

"[The] British mask is more efficient in delivering oxygen," he explains. "The Russian mask is a constant flow; the oxygen keeps coming into your mask. With the British one when you breathe out the valve closes and all the oxygen is captured in a bottle. When you breathe in again all the oxygen is coming through. You are not dependent on the flow rate so it is really efficient. The only problem with the British one is it is silicone, so when you take it off to eat or drink something, because it is wet, it can seal up and then people will start to panic because they are not getting oxygen. But if you just leave it on your mouth the breath will unseal it again."

Earlier today I sat in on a demonstration Dawa gave his clients on how to use their oxygen masks. There have been surprises here at Base Camp. One of the bigger ones is that most people have never used an oxygen mask before and the extent of the training they get is one hour on the day before they go up. Past Camp Three everyone will be on oxygen twenty-four hours a day until they come back down. The mask and the tank are critical to their survival above Camp Three unless they have acclimatized without it. Meagan is the only one I know here acclimatizing to climb without oxygen. And yet she knows more than any of the other clients who will be using it. Crazy shit. Arjun put his on backwards in the morning's demonstration.

Dawa's team is going for the twenty-third. "We're trying to avoid the big traffic jams, even if the weather is good," he says. "You can get stuck for two hours at Hillary Step—I want to avoid that."

I can see why. But I also know he can have all the intentions he wants—nobody is in charge here, nobody knows who is going up or when. As I get up to leave, he looks at me with a boyish smile and says, "Yeah, this is what it all comes down to: two months at Base Camp—forty days for some people." He laughs looking at me. "Then it's that one day, that one good day to stand on the top. You gotta make the right call and choose the right day."

After dinner I follow Carolina to an American group that includes a few folks from California and a woman from Poland celebrating her thirty-seventh birthday. Another woman in the group has been diagnosed with a rare, fatal disease. Their dome tent is like a five-star hotel with heaters and friendly people and dinner and birthday cake. We dance to Colombian music. After dinner their leader, Scott, tries to contact the Colombian team using his much more elaborate radio set-up. He connects to his Sherpa contacts on the mountain. Carolina is even more stressed. At a time when communication is so critically important, her satellite phone is still not working. They learn that not all of the Colombian team members will be going for the summit. Their team leader, Juan Pablo, is sick and will stay at Camp Three. Antonio is now at Camp Two and will hike down as he is also having health issues. But Nelson, Rafael and Albert have left Camp Four for the summit. Carolina has decided to spend the night in the American mess tent so she is close to a radio that works.

There is random kindness here. Despite the commercialization, the sacred is still alive. As I leave, they are just settling in to watch a movie. First class has privileges.

Walking back at night across the dark moraine and ice I get a bit lost for a while. Bashista and Childon are waiting and watching for me like worried parents when I arrive back at my camp at 11 p.m.

Chomolungma, my heart and prayers are with those on your breast: let them pass. Their hearts are full of love for you.

SUMMIT PUSH

At 3:30 a.m., Meagan leaves for the Lhotse summit.

Again, it is black outside as she packs up her things, drinks a cup of hot Tang and mentally prepares for her summit push. Only Meagan, her Sherpa guide, Pemba, and the cook are in the mess tent this morning. Nobody is saying much. Each replaces the batteries in their headlamps with fresh ones. You don't want that to burn out while hiking through the Icefall in the dark.

After a few minutes Dawa and Marshall join her in the mess tent as she puts on her harness. Dawa tells her: "They packed all the good chocolates for you, Meagan. Marshall and I are just going to be eating cashew nuts."

This raises a slight chuckle, but clearly Meagan is focused on what is ahead of her. Pemba is outside and ready so Meagan steps out into the cold, dark morning, tightens straps on her backpack, and double-checks the equipment on her harness.

Pemba tightens up his straps by the light of his headlamp; then he and Meagan put on their big backpacks and proceed to the puja. Pemba takes some rice from a small rock altar in front of the large puja where a bright flame burns. To the left a two-foot-high semicircle of rocks acts as a shelter for the fire. Pemba tosses some rice into the fire and Meagan begins her own ritual of walking around it. Now Pemba chants and throws rice over his shoulders and onto the rock altar. Megan closes her eyes, pats her heart a few times with a light fist, and says goodbye to Dawa and Apa. Dawa tells her he will give them a weather update about the peak later today. Meagan says they will call from Camp One. There's the light clang of climbing gear and the crunch of boots on frozen ice and moraine as two headlights disappear into the darkness.

At some point soon I will have to decide whether this trip needs to be extended to get the complete story, as May 27 is now being tossed around as a possible summit day. I decide to wait and see what Apa does.

Tomorrow the rest of my characters leave and the other half come back. Hard to believe we might leave in ten days. I've met many kind people. The challenges are within me—physical pain, emotional estrangement and spiritual uncertainties.

I worry for the safety of those I know. Many have summited today and are safely returning, but they are the more experienced climbers. Meagan is worried. I saw it in her this morning. The inexperienced climbers are not.

DAY 29: MAY 18

I wake to my forty-fifth birthday after a night filled with dreams—Brad Pitt at a party where I was in male drag with facial hair. Some scary men fighting with broken glass who I wanted to have thrown out of the party.

Andrew was up at 3:30 a.m. to film Apa getting up and prepping to take his clients up for the summit push. I peek out of my tent as he walks by in the dark. The only lights roaming about are headlights and the green Asian Trekking mess tent, which is lit up like a Japanese lantern amidst all the dark tents in the night. The puja is already burning juniper. When Apa walks into the mess tent, Marshall and Dawa are already there, getting a cup of tea from a hot Thermos. Dawa passes Apa some wrapped food to put into his knapsack. Apa fills his water bottle with orange Tang powder and warm water. Outside all the Sherpas are up before any signs of the clients. On the kitchen table is a book, *Men are from Mars, Women are from Venus.* As Apa gets ready Dawa sits down and starts to read the book. After a few minutes, Marshall asks, "Learn anything good?"

Dawa replies: "Yup, apparently women don't seek the same thing in relationships men do."

Both men laugh, and Dawa adds, "Probably true."

The joke is a bit of an icebreaker. Even Apa, with nineteen summits under his belt, looks a bit nervous. After some tea, he puts on his harness, and night slowly becomes day. Apa puts on his helmet and goes outside. It's cold but there's no wind and the skies are clear. Dawa follows him. As light breaks it seems everyone is now up at the Asian Trekking camp. The long-awaited day has arrived—summit time. The mood is sombre, as if all the climbers are having conversations with themselves in their heads. All the practice, all the work to get here, all the waiting, and now it's time. After just some tea most are ready to leave. Arjun and some of the climbers and their Sherpa guides pay their respects to the puja; others do not. Then all the clients shake Dawa's hand as he bids them good luck, and they launch into the Icefall.

The last to leave is Bags. Her Sherpa guide is putting her equipment on for her; she still has no clue. Dawa is visibly upset as he stands watching her with her arms held out as her guide puts on her climbing harness. Dawa says: "You're late."

"I know. I'm bad," she says. Bags takes her cellphone out of her pocket and hands it to Dawa, "Can you keep this for me?"

Dawa takes her phone and turns the power off. A ring tone goes off. It's a strange sound in this melody of shuffling down jackets and crunching footsteps on moraine and ice. "It's not good to be late in the mountains," Dawa says. Bags tells him she was talking on her cellphone to her mother all night because it is her mother's birthday. After Bags is dressed for the climb, she and her Sherpa guide leave—about twenty minutes later than the rest of the group—with Dawa's parting words: "Do what your Sherpa says, okay? Dig deep. Good luck."

After a pat on the back from Dawa, Bags disappears into the Icefall. For what seems like a long time Dawa, Marshall, Apa, Andrew and I watch as the clients and Sherpas move up the Icefall, so fragile and insignificant looking on the expansive canvas of the mountainside.

Dawa says, "There is a cyclone developing. I got a weather report yesterday. It won't be a problem with wind—it will be snow. Last year we had cyclone Aila, apparently this one is called cyclone Laila, so if it is like last year it is going to dump about four feet of snow in one day. It will more than likely be when everyone is back down at Base Camp. But if it is just developing now it will take a few days."

Apa has his photo taken by Marshall and some friends from Utah, and then goes to the puja for prayers before he too heads up the Khumbu Icefall.

Later that morning I give myself a birthday bath by hand with a metal bowl of hot water on a hard rock and a metal cup to scoop. It's the warmest day yet. I wash and brush my hair. It's amazing how the nights can be a psychological horror show and the days can be so full of kindness and laughter. No wonder light is associated with good, and people say, "Go to the light."

Once again I unfold the piece of paper that I've been carrying for five weeks, since the day Teresa departed Khumjung and returned to our life in Garden Bay. An eight-by-ten sheet of loose-leaf, neatly folded into a small square, a handwritten, tactile piece of her. A blue ink heart with the words "B-day message." After my hand bath I return to my tent to read it as I have already done so many, many times.

Happy Birthday Dee,

As I write this it is hard to fathom where you are upon reading it… hopefully closer to heaven and in good health. I'm so inspired by your tenacity to realize this dream despite the hardship involved in getting there: my short journey with you at the beginning of the trek was in relative luxury compared to where you were going when I left you in Khumjung. You are such an incredible woman and I thank you again for encouraging me to push myself to limits I previously doubted I was capable of achieving. It was great to partake in this project, even if only a short part of it, and to gain a better understanding of where you are and what you're doing… you often said to me, "Stop me if I ever get another crazy idea" or, "Don't ever let me do this again." You know I never will, right? I love you because you do follow your dreams, because you are not afraid, and because you trust in everything being as it should be (even if it's not what you think you wanted).

The letter is two pages of love, articulated just for me. As I read her words I know something has already changed in me. I know there are only a few weeks to go till my flight home, and I have never looked forward to a day more. But her love seems so far away. I fold the letter and put it back in my bra, where I have carried it since she gave it to me. And then I wipe the tears to hide my vulnerability from all the granite, ice and hard edges of Base Camp and go back to work to finish what I came here to do.

BASE CAMP CASINO

Moods are up at camp. Successful summits and more on the way. The Kazakh men are back and the Colombian team is coming down the mountain. It feels good to have some conclusion. Later, I will film the Kazakhstan team packing up. The beer their cook gave me for my birthday is chilling in the melting glacial ice.

I will spend many hours at the Asian Trekking camp in the next few days. The Colombians are having a party this afternoon. The climbers won't be down until tomorrow but many trekkers from Colombia have arrived at camp, including some of the team sponsors who did the trek as part of their own experience. I would say about thirty people have hiked in and the mess tent is becoming a barista bar. Rumour has it they will be serving iced coffees.

Not going to be a bad birthday.

The Latin music starts around 2 p.m. so Andrew and I grab two cameras and head out to the first real social event at Base Camp. Wind isn't too bad—cloudy and sunny skies. The first person we bump into is Comms John, the communication guy for the Canadian Crohn's team. He tells us the boys left for their summit push at 3:30 this morning. They are hoping for a May 22 summit.

"Coffee!" John exclaims. "The Colombians are having a celebration because two of their climbers made the summit yesterday, which is fantastic. Congrats to those guys, and it looks like Juan Valdez is one of these guys' sponsors." He points to a large red plastic banner that reads "Café Colombia." "So they are plying us with some coffee delicacies. There is actually iced coffee. I haven't seen this since Canada, so happy times."

This is by far the largest social gathering yet. The din of many people talking, the joie de vivre of the Colombian culture and the mug of Scotch on ice I am handed because Carolina knows it is my birthday make it a special and happy day. As I am being taught how to salsa dance in my big hiking boots, Andrew has a conversation with a Canadian climber who showed up alone a few weeks ago with really old climbing gear and an ambition to climb Everest. He is a small-framed older man, with grey hair and a short-cropped beard, blue eyes. There's something childlike in his nature. You know in *Star Trek* when a person from the past gets beamed on board the *Enterprise*? This guy looks like one of those. Almost like a ghost of climbers past.

Tom says he's from Quebec and he came here to commemorate his father, who piloted a B-24 Liberator over the top of Everest in 1944. "So one of the things I really wanted to do is to commemorate his presence up there with some Tibetan prayer flags. The prayer flags are there so that every time they flap in the wind you get a prayer that is sent off to the heavens, and it is returned to this auspicious planet we have in the form of rain, snow and it is the least we can do to bless this planet. Another reason is to show that geriatric people like myself should not be restricted from any of this sort of opportunity or activity. And if I can go and do this maybe I can be an inspiration to other people to go ahead and try things."

Tom has joined the season late in the game and didn't do the rotation system, but he is confident in his abilities. "I have climbed and so I have a reasonable idea what this body can do and will do. So for me two months' acclimatization is just a little too much. A five- to six-week schedule works better."

Tom isn't happy with the expedition company he paid to look after his logistics. They put him with the Colombian group, "even though I speak no Spanish," Tom says, and then he starts to cough. "Pardon me, the Khumbu silt cough." Tom has already been up as far as Camp Four, but he had to turn around then because his Sherpa guide's toes were frozen. Tom wants to go back up, but his guide has refused, and the company he hired says there is not enough oxygen for him to try again. But Tom says he is going up tomorrow, regardless. This is where things can get dangerous.

As Andrew and I leave the party, we bump into Antonio, who came down this morning because of some health issues above Camp Three.

"Well, I am a little bit disappointed because I don't stay on the summit, but my life is a more important thing, no? And when I came back, going down to Camp Three, and I see a Russian guy dead, in this moment I understand my decision is a really good decision. I like my friends made the summit. The purpose of this mission is complete, and all the Sherpas and my friends are alive and all my body is complete. I'm really young and the mountain will stay there and I try another time."

"That's smart, Antonio," I tell him. "The mountain is full of dead bodies from those who couldn't make that decision. What happened up there?"

"At 7,400 I don't feel my left body. I put oxygen and I tried to go higher and I have my oxygen at 1.5, and if I go to Camp Four with this pressure I don't summit because I don't have enough oxygen. So I put it at 1.0 point and I don't feel my…" He grabs and rubs his left arm. "I don't feel my hand, and at this point I decide to go down because I am risking my life and my team too because they try to help me and I decide to go down.

"This mountain taught me to be humble," he says, explaining that he and his teammate had trained very hard, doing a lot of climbing and dedicating themselves to this goal. They made it from Base Camp to Camp One in four hours whereas most people take six. They were feeling very strong, he tells me, adding, "But even if you are very strong or you feel that you are more capable than others up there, you see other people like Nelson, in a disability situation but stronger than you, in better shape, feeling better, that's a great lesson of humility.

"I also learned much from the people of Nepal: their attitude of service, how to be simple. People have a nice spirit, they are always happy. They have a tough life, the conditions they live in are not easy but they always have a smile on their face. Many times Western people complain about material things that we're missing, and you realize that's not so important for them. That's a very beautiful and worthy lesson."

For weeks now I have heard hollering and weird sort of karate "HUH" sounds coming from the Kazakh cook's tent. After a few hits of Scotch with

BASE CAMP CASINO

the Colombians, I decide to poke my head into the tent and find out what's going on. Risky, I know. On the ground of the tent is a dark blue fleece blanket, and on top of it, a round piece of leather sewn on top of a circular tin, and on top of that, two dice. Sitting around the dice are four Nepali men, all cooks and porters, each with a pile of beads like puka shells and a bunch of coins. I am in a Base Camp casino. When each takes their turn shaking the dice in a brown wooden box, they call out this loud "HUH" that builds in pitch until they slam the box and dice onto the leather drum. I observe from the tent door and decline an invitation to join them.

Next I poke my head into the Kazakh dining tent and find Max drawing pictures of the house he wants to build for his wife and children when he gets back home. He and two of the team members made it to the summit of Lhotse two days ago. He tells me he thought it was the most difficult of the many climbs they've done above 8,000 metres. They hit bad weather and were not properly equipped at Camp Four, having just a two-man tent for the three of them. At 3 a.m. they headed off for their summit push. The weather was good, Max said, clear and moonless, "which is to say it was still very, very cold. I don't know, maybe this was felt because we are older mountaineers, not so young anymore, but it was just very cold. And the route itself up to Lhotse has the characteristic of moving along a couloir. So even if somewhere around us there was sun, and mentally we understood that the sun had risen, there on the route, we were constantly in the shadows with wind howling."

He says as they approached the peak close to midday they weren't able to see the views because of fog. "We were in the clouds, snow was falling, and there were strong winds. Of course maybe in some ways this dulled our experience, our euphoria of standing on top of the peak, but in general we felt the accomplishment of finishing what we came here to do. Of course, most important of all was still to return back to Base Camp alive and healthy and only at the Base Camp, as per traditions of Kazakh mountaineering, could we shake each other's hands and congratulate one another with having summited the mountain." Max grins and looks at the drawing he's making of his house and then back at the camera. "We did

171

everything kind of simply, you know? So, some great things are done unceremoniously, with maximal effort being put into making sure you don't regret anything later.

"We completed a task that was begun by some of our eldest, eldest peers, the veterans of Kazakh mountaineering. We fulfilled the fourteen-peak plan with the national Kazakh team. The mountains have a very particular kind of atmosphere, where it's possible to feel when your loved ones are thinking about you out there, thousands upon thousands of kilometres away. This helps when you are on the mountain. Somewhere, beneath your heart, is located a photograph of your wife, your lover, your children. When you think about this it gives you pleasure. This is life." Max holds up his glass in a salute, and I turn off the camera.

After three hours of crazy Russian moonshine, I venture up the glacier with the camera. Moonshine gives courage. I see now why they drink the stuff. Hiking up with no ropes, no Sherpa and no permission, I make it through the maze of old rotting snow to the first aluminum ladder. The snow has the look and texture of old snow in late spring in Montreal, which I remember from living there in the 1980s. I set the camera at ground level to film the thick metal spikes of climbers' crampons as they cross the crevasse. I am there only a few minutes when the thunderous roar of a nearby avalanche has me up and running back down. Even moonshine can't overcome the fear of being buried alive.

NELSON VICTORIOUS

DAY 30: MAY 19

The rest of the Colombian team is returning today. To film them Andrew and I scramble a little way into the Icefall. We're following Carolina and two Sherpas as we hike between five-foot-high chunks of ice and the occasional boulder half-frozen in the ice that has entombed it for years. Andrew stops with Carolina, who is still coughing.

I continue a bit higher up the Khumbu Icefall. When I hear the hollering and whistling of those behind me, I know the team is on their final approach. After almost one week away, and now coming through the Icefall, they look exhausted and elated.

Carolina gives Nelson a big hug. He holds up a small Colombian flag for the camera, and suddenly it sounds like dozens of people hollering and whistling, and there's the sound of a drum and somebody playing a small green plastic harmonica. Nelson looks frail now with his artificial leg—almost in shock. This is the most action I have seen at Base Camp. Many of the corporate sponsor reps are here to welcome him and get into the photographs. Nelson looks like he is on the verge of tears. Everyone is hugging him and everyone else. Nelson seems particularly grateful to his Sherpa guide, Tongi. He has his arm around him, touches his face like a lover and cries as he hugs him. I cannot understand the words but their body language tells me they have been through something intense up there.

After group photos, Nelson's welcoming committee carries him on their shoulders to the Colombian media tent where he removes his artificial leg and waits for some chicken to be prepared for him. He sits on one side of the table with Rafael, while on the other side of the table numerous corporate reps anxiously await his stories.

Someone asks Rafael how he is doing, and he says he has a frostbitten toe and a sore neck. "I fell on the way down," he says. "I was coming down without oxygen, and I was alone. I didn't feel anything. When I could I moved forward along the rope and then I'd sit down and fall asleep. And then when I'd wake up, I'd look at the time on my watch and I had to keep on going down. The steps were very steep. I didn't see one of them. I missed the step and I fell over my backpack. It felt like a whiplash on my neck. And it was at night already. It was getting dark."

Nelson says, "When we went down, as we were the last ones, we couldn't find the oxygen bottles, because people who go down take desperately whatever they find."

Carolina asks, "So you didn't find the oxygen bottles that were at 8,500?"

Rafael and Nelson both respond, "There was nothing there!"

This is a common problem over 8,000 metres. When confronting death, people steal whatever oxygen they can to survive.

Nelson describes almost losing his prosthesis as he was rappelling down an ice wall. Both men look like they've stared death in the face. "We were extremely tired. I mean, people say, 'Everest, it's only a hike.' No! No. Every time you need to go with all these devices—the jumar, the carabiner. And you have just a small slip, you're done. And changing from one rope to another one, on a 50- to 55-degree ice wall, this small change is a big challenge. If you slip during the change, you fall down 1,000 metres. So, you enjoy it and you don't enjoy it. Because this is too close to the edge… I remember when we got to Camp Three for the first time that we slept there, Juan Pablo was getting in, I was already in, and suddenly he disappeared! Uhh! He fell into a crevasse! Up to his waist! So you are never, never safe. It's an amazingly beautiful and amazingly dangerous route."

"And how was the arrival to the summit?" someone asks.

"Oh no, before we got to the summit, we found a dead man, a Russian guy who had died and they were pulling him, so that makes you get shocked. The arrival to the summit was very beautiful but very long. We were waiting for it because there were a lot of people who had gone in the same window that we went, and they were there. In the Hillary Step, we had to wait forty minutes, one hour. That's why people die, waiting to cross. Besides, there are some parts of rock and ice, and rock and ice for people with two legs, it's very easy, because he steps hard, belays himself and goes, but I don't have sensibility in my leg, so for me it was really difficult—not to feel that my foot was well supported, and there were cliffs at both sides."

The tent is packed with people all listening to Nelson's every word. I am sitting on the floor right at his feet so I can point the camera up at him without other people getting into my frame. His prosthesis is lying on the ground in front of me. He looks so frail and small but at the same time the adrenalin of the experience animates his eyes and hands as he talks about the journey.

"The sunrise was precious, but I couldn't imagine what was at both sides, the super exposed ridge, the cliffs below, impressively beautiful. You should look at them for three seconds but not any more. If you spent more time looking, you would panic! The Hillary Step is a very, very scary place, because you need to climb up, sit on the ridge like riding a horse, turn at the side of the cliff and go forward. Extremely scary.

"I never thought it would be so hard, so difficult, nor [that] we should wait for so long, because of so many people in that moment. We thought we would arrive at 6 or 7 a.m. to the summit, but there were so many people! And also the weather window was not very wide. We thought it was going to be a two-, three-day window, but it was not like that. It was only a few hours' window.

"As we were climbing, some guides who were descending, I don't know who they were, said, 'No, turn back, the weather already changed and it's getting bad and dangerous.' We were close to the Hillary Step, and from there, it would be about two or three more hours to the summit. But no, no, we couldn't turn back. We were almost there and we trusted that we could make it."

PAIN IS WEAKNESS LEAVING

DAY 31: MAY 20

I wake up in the middle of the night for a pee and discover a foot of new snow. Snow is so quiet. I think about Marshall and his experiences in Iraq. I can't imagine six months in a war zone, counting the days with death on your shoulder. Here, the threat of death is either inside you—from the high-altitude—or on the mountain, from the daily avalanches and falling ice. I hear that a hurricane could hit us, four feet of snow in one day. Good grief. The weather-predicting game deserves its own chapter. Best quote I heard from a Sherpa: "Some reports say wind, some say no. I think we go and see for ourselves."

Ninety-two people summited Everest yesterday.

In the morning the sun is shining, and I have the pleasure of digging through really dirty laundry for the least dirty pair of socks I can find. Sore back. I think about how these small difficulties now feel like extreme challenges, and once again I consider the comfortable life that I—and most of the Westerners here—have come from: a life of luxury with big TVs, comfortable cars, furniture, bathrooms.

Base Camp is a weird place. Climbers cruise around like billboards with patches of corporate sponsors sewn on to their clothes. More patches are stuck onto their tents. I tried to find sponsors too, but ended up borrowing against my equity. When I look at the multipatched clothes of the people around me, I think our bodies have become commercialized and wonder if our spirits have too.

Marshall and Dawa are sitting in their communication tent, where they will spend most of their time until everyone on the team is down safely. They are both staring at a weather forecast on the laptop, Marshall stroking his beard and Dawa inches from him wearing a buff over his mouth, eyes focused on the screen. They are trying to determine the best day for the summit. Sounds like May 23. Dawa takes his buff off, grabs the satellite phone and calls up to Camp Two.

"It looks like a cyclone is developing over the Bay of Bengal," he tells us. "Luckily it seems it is going to be moving away from us, to the east, rather than coming at us. This is good news. I am a little bit worried about snow, because with a cyclone comes a lot of precipitation and not so much that the precipitation will affect us on the summit day, but rather when we come down and especially when we are packing up and leaving Base Camp. If everything is covered in snow it is going to be a lot of work for my staff. And it is just real crap at the end of the season, you know.

"Everybody seems to be aiming for the twenty-second and twenty-third right now—other expeditions as well. That gives me more confidence because they are getting different weather reports, but also with more people up there they can also support each other should things go wrong."

Apparently Bags left Camp Two with the team this morning but turned around because she wasn't feeling great. Dawa says the good news for her is that the best weather window has moved so she still has time on her side.

"We give her the support and everything," Dawa explains, "but at the end of the day it is her that has to put one foot in front of the other. She has to get herself up there."

The same weather window will be true for Meagan as well. Everest and Lhotse are practically the same mountain; they share the same ridge.

"Lhotse is a little bit more sheltered than Everest because you climb in a couloir," explains Dawa. "Lhotse is more dangerous if it snows. There are certain sections on the route that have to be fixed; the rope is not completely fixed. So I am sending a Sherpa with rope a day ahead of Meagan.

He and some other Sherpas from ING are going to fix the ropes. Again, Meagan is climbing without oxygen so she is more susceptible to cold injuries and the wind is something we have to watch for. Meagan has two Sherpas with her, and they are going to be carrying extra oxygen, emergency oxygen, so in case Meagan does face difficulties she can get on oxygen and come back down."

Not far from my tent some porters are bashing tin cans in big white bags with a big metal mallet. Other guys are crushing cans by hammering them with heavy flat rocks. Recycling at 5,000 metres. When I look up and see little specks of black, the people climbing up the Khumbu Icefall appear as fragile as the tin cans, the mountain as ruthless as the eight-pound steel mallet.

FINAL INTERVIEWS WITH THE COLOMBIANS

Juan Pablo

The Colombians are leaving today, so Andrew and I catch up with Juan Pablo and Nelson for final interviews before they leave. We find Juan as he finishes packing up his personal belongings just outside his sleeping tent. He has a bad cough and looks ten years older than he did a week ago. He is sick, and visibly worn down. His face looks swollen. He tells me he made the decision to send only two climbers to the top because they didn't have enough oxygen and one of their Sherpa guides got sick. So Nelson and Rafael were chosen. All was well until two communication errors nearly proved fatal. First the Sherpa carrying Rafael's oxygen and following behind him turned around without telling Rafael he was going back. Second, when Rafael ran out of oxygen and radioed Juan Pablo to ask what had happened and what he should do, he was at the South Summit, but Juan Pablo thought he was at the Hillary Step.

Juan says, "Rafa gave me the wrong information. He was instead close to the South Summit, and way too far from the main summit, as he thought. It means that he spent about four more hours with a lack of oxygen, which implied that he spent a lot of energy, and during the descent it started to be evident, because of the impact of having used oxygen and then having to stop using it. But in that moment I didn't know because communication was very difficult. I didn't know what was going on exactly. I only knew that they hadn't reached the summit at 7:20 a.m.—what we were expecting if they were at the Hillary Step when they called—but later, through some information coming from Camp Two, I knew they had summited at 11:20 a.m. and at 11:50 a.m., so they started to descend very late."

Thinking they would need to rescue the two, Juan eventually went with Jangbu Sherpa and four bottles of oxygen. They met them twenty or thirty minutes from Camp Four and returned safely to camp. Rafael had almost lost his life, but they had reached the summit and their objective was accomplished.

Nelson

Although he looks thinner and tired, Nelson has that same sense of peace I remember in Ani Choying in Kathmandu. As their camp is being dismantled around us we set up a folding chair on the broken rock and ice for Nelson to sit on to film his final interview. I ask him to describe the final push from Camp Four to the summit. He tells me they got to the camp on May 16 at 5 p.m. at which point the summit attempt was in question because there was a bad storm with high winds at Camp Four. The weather forecast said it would improve, but time passed and Juan Pablo told them if the winds didn't ease by 9:30 p.m. they would not leave for the summit. But others left in the middle of the storm, so at 9:30, they decided to go. They were the last of a line of about forty or fifty people. This raised their spirits, he said, but they also knew they were late and the last, and that it would likely give them problems at the Hillary Step.

"But we left. The night was really tough: it was not windy but it was cold. I didn't know how the prosthesis and my leg would respond with so much cold, and step by step, time was passing by—11 p.m., 12 a.m., 1 a.m., 2 a.m. Human beings usually suffer from a kind of lapse between 11 p.m. and 3 a.m., and it's difficult, because it's the time when your body is usually sleeping, so you feel anxious that you will fall asleep. I thought I was not going to make it, but I remembered my situation when I was at the hospital [for almost nine months]. And I remembered when I was lying over this kind of hammock to hold the pelvis with the other parts of my body, and I thought that if I had resisted so many months hanging there, feeling the strongest pain of all, I could resist everything that night.

"And I thought, the sunrise will come. And at 4:30 a.m., the sun started to rise and glow over the peaks around, like small gold gems. That was spectacular! I could see the other people there, and I could see that I still had the probability, and that I hadn't frozen."

I once read that pain is weakness leaving. Despite looking frailer I can see Nelson's spirit is calmer and stronger. The apprehension before the climb has been replaced with the satisfaction that comes from succeeding.

Nelson smiles and continues. "Many people were turning around because the night was very cold, but I was in perfect physical condition. And, well, it was slowly dawning, dawning, and I could see the valleys to Tibet and to Nepal. And something very important, and which I'm thankful of—it's the human strength, as in, for example, Dorje Sherpa. He was an angel for me. He was always there by my side. He always asked me if I had oxygen, if I was warm, if I had any problem. I think without them [the Sherpas], we wouldn't have reached our objectives."

Nelson shifts a little, then says, "There were traffic jams along the way, at the bottleneck of the Hillary Step. We were there for almost an hour, waiting for them to climb. It was amazing. Everything could happen. We could have been trapped in a storm and [frozen] there, but there was something inside of me, something very deep, which was telling me that it wouldn't happen, that we were going to make it. But a Sherpa who was going down with one client from a commercial expedition said, 'Please, turn back. There's a storm coming and you can only get to the Hillary Step. There are a lot of people waiting to go up.' But it was not like that. We could resist almost an hour in the Hillary Step, waiting for them to let us continue. When we got to the summit, I felt many mixed feelings.

"I started crying. I remembered so [much] time that I had spent at the hospital, when I had to leave my leg in order to reach my dream. Because this dream, the summit of Mt. Everest, was depending on this: my foot. If

180

I would keep it, I couldn't go back to the mountain. If I would leave it and take a prosthesis, I could conquer my dreams.

"I believe that sometimes you need to let go of material things in order to reach the highest ideals in your life. You can't keep the problems all your life only because you are not able to let go of them. So this is when it comes to the 'ritual' to leave my leg, which I call 'the detachment ritual,' and it is about releasing the things that are hurting me, that don't let me be happy. Instead of saying they hurt me, they don't let me be happy—okay, let's leave it. And there was no return point. It never got to my mind the idea of not doing it. I was completely convinced that I should do it, and it had to be in that exact moment.

"There are people who believe that if they're missing a finger, a leg, an eye, they can't go back to work anymore, they can't be the same person again. No, I think I was not only representing Colombia, but the whole world. Because disability is only mental. Failure is not a consequence of falling down, it's only a lack of will to stand up again. Gandhi said, when a man suffers—again and again—hits, frustrations, bankruptcy, failures, those are only a sum of his experiences which will result in success. Yes, the mountain has revealed so many things this time. It has made me see that we human beings are very small, and mountains are very big. What it has given to me, and what it has revealed: the secret of humility. To feel smaller every time, and to feel bigger every time. This is a revelation of humility and greatness. Completely, it has changed me."

It's clear the summit and the struggle have given Nelson some peace. It is hard not to be inspired by his story. He shows no arrogance or ego. And I am reminded that reality is an interpretation. I came with the idea to make a film about the shadow of Everest: the commercialization, the ecological destruction, the meaninglessness of it all. The idea of climbing a mountain with lineups has absolutely zero appeal to me. I go into the mountains to feel alone, to get away. And I have never paid a dollar to find that space and peace in nature. That is part of what gives it value and meaning: a complete contrast from living in a society where everything is about making money and buying what you need. But I can see the mountain had a different meaning for Nelson, and the lineups and commercialization had no effect on his dream. I am reminded of something Ani said in Kathmandu. In response to one of my questions about Buddhism, she replied, "That's how you see it from the outside, but that is not exactly how it is because I am in it myself."

The first time I came to Base Camp, in 2007, I was an observer, seeing it from the outside for just a few hours. What I saw was the darkness. With this second trip I have become part of Base Camp, and now I see it from the inside.

Enlightenment is defined in the dictionary as "a blessed state in which the individual transcends desire and suffering and attains Nirvana." I believe Nelson has at least momentarily achieved that state. I, however, am still far from it.

After wrapping up the final interviews with the Colombian and Kazakh teams, I head back to my dining tent for dinner feeling tired and cranky. I would love to be alone but I need to transfer footage, check on camera batteries for tomorrow and have dinner. Miloh serves dinner as soon as I arrive and within minutes Bashista is eating with his mouth open. He always does, but tonight it grates on me and I can see it grates on Andrew too. So after I ask Bashista to pass me a pappadum, I ask him about gay rights in Nepal.

"Very wrong, very bad, everybody here thinks so, very bad." He looks directly at Andrew and says, "Right? Very bad."

Andrew replies, "No, actually, many of my friends in Canada are gay. I don't think there is anything wrong."

Bashista looks surprised by Andrew's answer. "No, really? I don't think it's good."

And then I speak. "I'm gay, Bashista," I tell him. "You know Teresa, that woman we travelled with partway here that you like so much. She's my wife."

He points his finger in my face. "You are very bad lady," he says. "Very, very, very bad lady."

I clench my jaw, my hands make sweaty fists beneath the dinner table and I say, "Well, remember this, buddy. I am the woman with the tip money. And right now, there might not be a tip for you."

Bashista gets up and walks out of the tent. My heart is pounding but I take deep breaths. He is a government official, and I have to get out of here with equipment and film safely. Anger never changes a person's mind. Can't say it won't come out again, though. It's a river of blood that runs through me and sometimes if I block it the dam breaks. It just came very close to breaking.

A bad thunder and lightning storm moves in. The dreams and aspirations of all my characters are at Camp Two. I hope the mountain is feeling kind. I know I am not.

MILLION-DOLLAR QUESTIONS

DAY 32: MAY 21

I have my first pee-bottle experience in the night. Until now, the thought of messing up has been motivation enough to drag my ass out of the tent every night. But this time I wake up with maybe a minute to relieve myself, and peeing in the bottle seems better then peeing in my long johns. I quickly push my sleeping bag over to the side and discover it's kind of like peeing in a bottle for a doctor. It's fine. And it makes me wish I'd got on that program thirty-four days ago. I put the bottle outside my tent and climb back into my sleeping bag.

With no watch and no sense of what day it is, it's hard to know when to get up. I take my cue from bright sunshine on the tent and the delivery of the small bowl of water to wash my face and hands. That is the 7 a.m. get-out cue. Miloh isn't even up yet, though, so it must be not quite 6. I leave my tent door open so I can see the soft blue light of dawn on the big peaks.

It feels colder. The climbers should be at Camp Three now, ready for the summit window today. In her final interview, Carolina said now we know many of the people on the mountain, and she was right. It's hard not to worry and wonder as I look up.

10 A.M.

The Colombians are gone. It took just a few hours for their camp to be folded and packed. Andrew and I filmed them as they embarked on the trail out after a light breakfast and a closing prayer around the puja. This isn't a place you hang around once the job you came for is done.

I'm hoping some more of my characters will summit tomorrow. Camp is smaller and quieter today: two hundred climbers and as many or more Sherpas are all up the mountain. Some tents have been dismantled, some yaks are packed. Andrew and I are both counting the days.

4 P.M.

Miloh, Childon and I drink beer in the afternoon. Bashista and Andrew abstain. Childon helped get it through the underground economy. It took a couple of hours, but the businessman came back with a six-pack, some Pringles and a dead chicken. Beer costs 250 rupees each, approximately four dollars. But I am still cranky and hope a few drinks will take the edge off.

Apparently 150 people are going for the summit tonight and tomorrow night. Busy.

Comms John at the Canadian tent told me earlier in the day that only Rob made it to Camp Three. The other two turned around and went back to Camp Two, both fighting stomach flu. This is not great news for Rob. John is stressed.

After dinner I go to get an update and as I walk into their dining tent I see Comms John sitting alone staring at the satellite radio in his hand. I can tell he's pissed off. He stares right at me. Somehow his red beard, red down jacket and red plaid hat emphasize his look of frustration.

"Rob is at Camp Three today, tomorrow to Camp Four, leave at 9 p.m. for the summit next morning—maybe. He's bummed. I can hear it in his voice. As he said to me earlier today, 'I never thought I would be sitting here alone waiting, you know, and I understand I can't just sit here. If I sit here for twenty-four hours it could cost me the summit.' He's battling his own personal demons tonight."

There is a pause. Comms John looks like he is going to cry. Then he says, "But he is going to be with probably the strongest Sherpa on the mountain so he is all good." Silently, he goes back to looking up the mountain, then at his radio, waiting for more contact from Rob.

8 P.M.

Tonight I piss off Bashista some more by shooting back Russian moonshine in the dining tent, a present bestowed on us by the departing Kazakhstan team. With Bashista, it's like I'm hanging with the Hindu equivalent of an evangelical Christian. He glares at me as I shoot back a shot and then bang the glass on the table, observing the Kazakh tradition, of course. I just smile and look him straight in the eye, and he storms off to eat in the cook's tent. I don't like people trying to control me. I was born with a built-in aversion to authority. My mother calls it learning everything the hard way.

The skies are grey, and the wind picks up as I make my way back to my tent. I decide the moonshine stays on the table until we leave.

DAY 33: MAY 22

I spend most of the day over at the Asian Trekking communication tent where Dawa and Marshall are still spending all their time. Both are in good spirits. "I was telling him how unmanly Mormon men are," Marshall turns and says to me as I walk in. "In the tradition, it's really okay to cry. It's expected sometimes, and using violence is pretty unacceptable, or contention in any way is not acceptable." Still looking at me, he says with a big smile, "And nobody drinks, right. That's why I was so fascinated with the Finns." Now laughing, "These hard-drinking manly men, it was awesome, ha ha."

I say I thought they were being overly optimistic bringing four hundred condoms to Base Camp. We all laugh.

It's interesting sitting here with a Buddhist Sherpa and a Mormon American, especially when the conversation turns to God. Marshall says, "Dawa thinks that as a theist, I have to prove that God exists; otherwise I can't be a theist. And I disagreed. The conclusion was that if I am telling him that he has to believe in God then I have to provide proof. But if I am only saying that I believe in God, I don't have to provide any proof."

"Basically what he is saying is because he believes in God, he exists," says Dawa.

Before the debate continues, Arjun's cellphone rings. Dawa picks it up and goes outside. I can hear, "Hello, Captain..." as he leaves. Marshall cracks a big smile and says Arjun's father has been calling a few times a day since Arjun left for the summit. I ask Marshall what he thinks about Base Camp now that he is getting near the end of his stay. He has spent as much time here as I have.

"You know, it's been really good. There have been a few hours on a few days that I have been bored."

I ask him the question I have been asking everyone. "Do you think if you commercialize the sacred it loses its meaning?"

Marshall replies, "I think if people commercialize the sacred then it loses its meaning for them, but it doesn't lose it for me. I think about Apa because he gets a lot of sponsors, but I don't think it changes for him personally. This whole place is spiritual. I have learned a lot, I think I have grown a lot. It was my intent to come here and change. It has been a good environment to become a better person, because it is very austere, not comfortable. There is a lot of time for reflection. This place was made for reflection."

I tell Marshall the climbers I have talked to at Base Camp who have done the fourteen highest peaks all tell me the other mountains aren't commercialized to this extent. They don't have a thousand people lining up to climb; they don't have dozens of companies taking up paid clients. They tell me this is an anomaly. I ask Marshall what he thinks the prime motivation is for people to climb Everest.

"I think there is something special about Mt. Everest that draws everybody here more than any other mountain and it is sort of obvious, because it is the tallest mountain in the world. But there is something about that. I think people feel an ownership of it even though they are not from Nepal; it's like everybody's mountain. The second-highest mountain, well that's Nepal's mountain, but the highest point on earth, that's everybody's. There is a fascination and a draw to it. That's why trekkers come here just to get a peek of it; you don't get that on any other mountain."

It's true. Like pilgrims going to Mecca, an average of 40,000 people a year trek to Base Camp just to see it for an hour or two. We talk about how the peak of Everest has become the world's highest stage. I tell him, "It's sort of like a soapbox. If you get to the top you can say something to the world." I mention the people I've met, people who are dying, people who have lost a limb, people who are sick.

"The act of mountaineering is inherently selfish," Marshall says. "And a lot of people try to make it look differently, but really what you are doing is getting to the top of the mountain because you want to get to the top of the mountain. It doesn't do any good for anybody else except for you. It's pretty selfish. That is why so many people try to attach something to it, attach a higher purpose to it."

Dawa walks back into the tent just as the radio goes off with bad news. Strong winds at Camp Four destroyed two of the four Asian Trekking tents. Dawa looks less relaxed as he says, "If the clients have to stand around in the wind that could spell serious trouble."

By evening, the tent walls are blowing and there is a green tinge to everything from the camera light reflecting off them. Someone has moved the propane heater into the tent to make it more bearable. Marshall is sitting on a folding lawn chair with his big orange and black parka on, hands in pockets, a foot in front of the heater. Every hour he files a Twitter update on Apa's progress up the mountain.

"The Twitter feedback today from Apa's blog has been incredible," he says. "It has been fun but I am pretty tired right now. Bagyashree is coming down. She is not going to make it. She couldn't walk yesterday so she is back at Camp Two and coming down today. I haven't put it on the blog yet. I want to let her tell her family, want to be respectful to her feelings."

Dawa is worried about Meagan. After trying numerous times to contact her from the communication tent, he has again bundled himself up and gone outside with a satellite phone. "Meagan, Meagan, Meagan. This is Dawa Steven, do you copy?" He shouts to Marshall to try and reach her from the radio inside the communication tent. It takes a while, and Dawa becomes increasingly agitated.

Finally a little voice comes through—it's Meagan. She tells Dawa there is not enough rope for the unroped sections. Dawa does his best to help them decide how to handle the situation. "Just past a dead body, 20 metres before the couloir, there is some rope," he says to Meagan, and then tells us: "If they can make it up to the rope or if they have a rope they can go up just for the 40 metres to the fixed line. After the fixed line it is almost completely fixed, plus there is a deposit of 100 metres of rope. And they only need about 70 metres in the couloir to fix. So the million-dollar question is: can they make it 40 metres to the fixed line? Also bearing in mind that Meagan is without oxygen and we have got to be extra careful. That is the big question."

Two of the Bad Finns are also trying to climb Lhotse and are thinking of turning around. They are climbing with Meagan but have no Sherpas of their own, and although they are very strong, according to Dawa they are not really experienced mountaineers, so it's probably a good decision for them to turn back. But it's hard on Meagan's morale, as well as the Sherpas'.

Dawa says, "The problem here is that because the Finns are afraid to go up, nervous about going up, that also infects the rest of the team. They start getting more afraid than they should be, and they stop thinking clearly, rationally. Right now I'm telling them to just take it easy, calm down and see what they can do because right now from Base Camp I can do nothing. The problem solving has to happen up there. All I can do is give them the information I got according to what the Kazakhs told me about the fixed rope, where the deposited rope is."

The wind has picked up on the mountain this evening. Dawa is worried. If there is no rope, the climbers are not moving and the winds are blowing against them, which he calls a recipe for disaster. Dawa walks outside with his radio. "Camp Two, Camp Two, Camp Two, over." There is no reply. "Nothing." He shakes his head in frustration. "For some reason, we are not getting radio signals today. Camp Two , Camp Two, Camp Two, over."

THE UNEQUAL MOUNTAIN

DAY 34: MAY 23

Andrew spends the early morning hours filming Marshall, Dawa and Chunu in the communications tent. Marshall and Chunu sleep in their chairs, heads nodding, leaning forward as they doze. Dawa is semi-awake, holding a satellite phone in his hand. The sides of the tent flap and shake in the cold wind. Most of the team have left Camp Four and are somewhere in the dark, climbing for the summit.

At 4 a.m. Marshall wakes up for his hourly update on Facebook and Twitter. His eyes half-slits, he has hardly slept all night. He gets up from the folding lawn chair he has been dozing in and looks over Dawa's shoulder at the equipment.

Dawa says, "The weather is not the best. They have predicted the higher range to be higher than we originally thought. The lower range is about the same. That's not good news for me considering my guys are all the way up on the mountain. Temperatures are lower by about five degrees; wind is the issue. I'm trying to figure out what is going to happen with the wind today. When the sun comes up the wind should die down according to the trends, and it starts to pick up again in the afternoon. So generally the climbers climb through the night and in the early morning when they have the lowest range of the winds. As they summit and come back down the winds start to pick up, but by that time they are not even there. My Sherpas said the winds picked up a little bit, and Meagan didn't sound too stressed out but in Base Camp we are getting quite a bit of wind. I am getting a little bit nervous because of what I am seeing here with my own eyes." Dawa stands up, puts on his gloves, the hand-held mic for his phone clipped onto his North Face jacket collar, a wool toque on his head.

"If the winds prove to be really ugly, Meagan for sure has to come back down—she is without O's. The other climbers are with a good team. They are with eight Sherpas including Apa. Unless it is something that can blow you off the mountain, they can keep going. The important thing is that they keep moving and stay warm."

Marshall sits down in front of the laptop and asks Dawa where he thinks Apa is right now.

"Somewhere between the South Summit and the balcony," Dawa replies, then goes outside to try to contact Camp Two from another location. He comes back ten minutes later to confirm that Arjun and Apa are on the South Summit, and that they are about an hour from the peak. The rest are about two hours away.

A few moments later, we find out that Meagan has decided to come back down. She and one of her two Sherpas, Kameii, decided that the 40-metre unroped section was too dangerous so they turned around and are now at Camp Four, where they will rest for the whole day. Today there will be more teams going up and that means there will be a lot of rope up there, so it should be easy for someone to fix that section. She will stay at Camp Four until the unroped sections can be fixed, and will try again for the summit, but she will have to forget about trying to do it without oxygen.

Dawa is concerned about how Meagan is going to do, considering she has already exerted herself. She has to wait for other people to come up so the rope can be fixed, and she has just one emergency bottle of oxygen to get back down. Dawa decides to bring Kameii down. He was only there to help Meagan on the unroped sections. Kameii has some spare bottles of oxygen and may be able to leave some for Meagan and Pemba to share.

Dawa jokes that his Sherpa dialect skills are weak. When he hears them on the phone talking to one another it stresses him out because if they yell to be heard over the wind it always sounds like something is going wrong. "The annoying thing is, I'll be like 'Naga, Naga, what's happening?' And he will say something like, 'The Sherpas are at Camp Three, it's all good, the wind is not that strong, they are just having a cup of tea.' And I'll be like, 'Bastard! Can you just talk in a little bit of a calmer voice on the radio?'" Dawa laughs. "This is one of the things to get me to speak Sherpa better."

Marshall agrees. "There are some people on the radio that sound like the world is ending." He mimics someone talking gibberish loud and fast. "I have no idea what they are saying but it sounds like they are freaking out. And then there is some guy who always sounds like he is about to die." In a slow, laboured way, Marshall says, "H-e-l-l-o b-a-s-e-c-a-m-p . . ."

"That's Ang Dawa," Dawa says, and they both laugh. "In my opinion the reason the Sherpas talk so loud on the radio—they also do that on the phone—[is that] when telephones first came into the country the connections were so terrible you had to shout. It's the same with my father. When I talk to him he shouts down the phone." Dawa asks Marshall to turn down the radio so he doesn't have to hear them talking to each other.

At 6:33 a.m. the radio goes off. Arjun and Apa are now on the summit. Dawa is relieved. "I told Arjun not to stay long, to take a few pictures, then come back down safely, because that is more important." Apa will stay up longer to take pictures for his sponsors.

Dawa grabs Arjun's cellphone and goes outside into the early morning where the skies are clear but the wind is roaring. "Hello, hello, Captain Vajpai?" Dawa says into the cellphone. "Good morning, sir. This is Dawa Steven, do you hear me? Congratulations! Your son is the youngest Indian to summit Mt. Everest. He just summited two minutes ago. The rest of the team is on its way. Arjun is there right now. He will be there for ten minutes taking pictures and so on and then he will head down. Yes, yes, you can call back in two minutes, but if I don't answer try again in five minutes because I am waiting for the rest of the team to summit, so my priority is for the rest of the team to be there safely, and if you call during that time I won't answer. Oh, okay, Captain Vajpai. Congratulations again."

Dawa looks into our camera and says, "Makes it all worth it." A brief smile, then back on the radio, concerned again.

Marshall, sitting in front of his laptop, types into Apa's blog, all in capital letters, "APA HAS SUMMITED EVEREST TWENTY TIMES! NEW WORLD RECORD!!!!!!"

Dawa hums, visibly much happier. Marshall, looking at his social media feeds, says, "This is just exploding." Dawa calls his father and in a stream of Nepali sprinkled with "congratulations" tells him Apa has just summited.

Marshall says, "It just keeps on going. This is awesome. This is the most exciting thing I have ever tweeted."

Andrew, still filming, asks Dawa what people feel like once they come down off the mountain. Are they feeling elated or are their emotions more complicated?

"When they first come down the mountain it hasn't hit them yet. It is just a lot of physical hardship. They haven't distinguished yet between reaching Camp Four, reaching the balcony, reaching the summit, because it is all hard. It is all about putting one step in front of the other. When they come down here they sort of don't know what they've just done. It is only once they get back home and with friends and family that they realize what an achievement [it is]. Initially it hasn't hit them yet, and it won't. They come back down and they are like, 'Hey, hello,' it feels just like another rotation. They will be happy, of course. There's a lot of relief, but they won't be proud quite yet. It is only when they get back home they will be like, 'Gee, I was on the highest mountain in the world.'"

CANADIAN TEAM

Over at the Canadian tent, I get an update on Rob. Bazu, the head Base Camp Sherpa and Sirdar, is sitting at the entrance of his tent. Over his satellite radio I can hear Guide John saying, "Bazu, we are missing five or six bottles of oxygen."

"Oh, very sad. What to do? Maybe we have enough oxygen. What you think?" Bazu says.

Comms John says, "This morning Rob got up at Camp Three with two Sherpas and they climbed into Camp Four, and it is the first time in a few days anybody from our team has been to Camp Four since they did the original oxygen drop. So when they did their inventory as they ordinarily would, Teng Doje found that we were missing six bottles. It looks like another team probably ran out of O's and decided to borrow, or 'take' would be the correct term."

This is the shadow of the ambition. Many bottles will be stolen above Camp Four as they are every year. I wonder how many of the dead bodies up there died because someone stole their oxygen. And is that not a form of manslaughter? But I get it. If I felt myself dying up there my honour would fall behind my need to live. When my fight-or-flight response gets activated, I go into preservation of self, completely disconnected. It is horrible. It is dark. And it is in most of us. That is why it is so hard to look at.

The good news for Comms John amidst the bad news is that their weather forecast for tomorrow looks like sun and less wind. "Fortunately cyclone Laila headed east over India so she will spare us her fury."

Dawa thinks it is going to snow. I hope their forecast is right. A cyclone and four feet of snow are not what anyone here needs now.

Comms John says, "The cyclone everybody has been worried about is nowhere near us and is only getting weaker. In fact, it is not a cyclone anymore—it is being characterized as a tropical depression, so it looks like we are going to have four or five good days of weather. It sounds like Rob has decided to stay put for a night in Camp Four. He wants to wait for John and Darrell to come up so the three of them can summit as a team. It is a little bit of a risky move for him because he is at 8,000 metres in the South Col and he is not really breathing much in the way of oxygen. He is going to be on low-flow bottled oxygen for the next twenty-four hours before they start climbing. So he could get tired, but it is something that is really important to him, to be part of this team and to have this team with him. He has weighed his options and made his decision."

Minutes later it is confirmed over the satellite phone that they have twenty-six bottles in South Col, and the problem has been solved. Asian Trekking has given them five of their extra oxygen bottles now that their clients have summited and are coming back down. The Canadians will give them five full ones at Base Camp. The plan is for Guide John and

Darrell to be at Camp Four tomorrow by noon with a summit push as a team tomorrow night.

Comms John explains more about the oxygen dilemma to us. "The mountain is not equal. There are a lot of people who came unprepared and they did it because of money, and they think they are okay. They think they are going to breathe O's at 2 litres per minute, and that's going to give them seven hours. It is a fourteen-hour round trip from South Col, so they figure they only need two bottles and one for South Col for sleeping, so they go with three bottles. The big teams have a minimum of five bottles per client; a lot of them have seven bottles per client. And it is not because they are overprepared. It is because their clients are climbing and sleeping with higher flow rates, which is a lot safer."

Later, in their mess tent, Comms John will tell Bazu he wants the word to get out that they are offering two hundred dollars to anyone who knows who stole their oxygen. Guide John also tells Teng Doje to ask around up on the mountain. They know there is nothing they can do but they want to know who stole it.

DECISIONS

DAY 35: MAY 24

Another rough night with a bad gut, liver and back. I feel like I haven't slept an hour and wake up feeling awful. That's it—no more booze till I'm home. Can't forget the effects of high-altitude.

I need a bowel movement, too—it has been days, but the bucket in the latrine tent is past the full point and now the excrement is on the rocks around the top. The surface is unstable. I have nightmares about the rocks giving way and falling into the bucket of shit. I think dying from an avalanche would be better because at least it would be cleaner. The smell in there triggers my gag reflex even with my handkerchief embalmed in peppermint essential oil.

I smell burning juniper, which means something: a summit, a prayer for good weather, a sign, sign, everywhere a sign. A few more filming days, a few more sleeps, then a 96-kilometre walk into a Maoist rebellion.

After a few hours of transferring footage, I join Max in the Kazakh tent for a beer and some fried black bread with an old retired climber who used to be their military commander. I know, I know, I said no more booze. But you can't hang out with a Kazakh and not drink. They insist. It is almost like taking a vow of trust. The two men have stayed behind to wait for the body of Sergei, their teammate who died last year, to come down the mountain. The body will be carried down by eight Sherpas and then buried in Gorak Shep. As I walk into their dining tent, I find them sketching again, still designing the house Max will build for his wife and kids in Almaty.

10:00 A.M.

Any moment now Arjun and Apa will be coming down the Khumbu Icefall back into Base Camp. Andrew and I are set up at the base of the Icefall to film their return and we are both brimming with the happy idea of departure. You know the old saying, "It's been fun and it's been real, but it hasn't been real fun."

Outside Dawa's tent, Dawa is pacing with a satellite phone awaiting word of Meagan. She went on oxygen after spending an extra night at Camp Four and is now on the summit push with Pemba. Clear skies, no wind. After the struggle getting past the unroped sections beyond Camp Four, all our fingers are crossed for her. After a half-hour or so, there is action on the phone. It is all in Nepali, but I hear "oxygen, no oxygen," and Dawa is smiling. Meagan has summited Lhotse.

Dawa switches to English, talking and pacing back and forth. "Great, great," he says into the phone. "Come back down as soon as possible, and keep your wits about you because the way down is more tricky than the way up. Over."

Meagan's voice comes over the phone loud and clear for us all to hear: "Yeah, I will definitely take my time on the way down 'cause, uh, I can see how it will be very tricky. Over."

"All right, well, enjoy. Congratulations once again, and we are all waiting for you for a party." Dawa smiles at me, and I give a holler and shout out, "Congrats, Meagan!"

After that Dawa wanders off for more conversations in Nepali. With the team all on their way down, the process of dismantling Camp Four can soon begin. Logistics and manpower kick in. But about fifteen minutes later, he returns, looking up at the Khumbu Glacier. "There's Apa and Arjun, with his red boots and his grey trousers and his long shaggy hair."

For a while we watch their two small figures get closer until finally they come out of the ragged ice sculptures. Andrew is there waiting with the camera rolling as Apa looks at Arjun and says, "Here we are at Base Camp, all our fingers and all our toes."

Dawa comes running across the fragmented rock scree and ice with another Sherpa, both carrying yellow silk scarves to place on their shoulders and around their necks. The scarves are part of a Tibetan tradition and are given at births, at wedding ceremonies and when people leave or come back from a journey. They symbolize purity and compassion. After putting the scarf on Apa, Dawa embraces Arjun in a big hug and tells him, "Good job, good job. I spoke to your father yesterday. He is so proud of you. Call him in a few minutes, okay?"

Minutes later the kitchen staff shows up with a tray of mugs and a kettle filled with steaming hot water and Tang. Quickly two mugs are filled and given to Apa and Arjun and just as they start to sip them, a huge avalanche begins near the edge of the Khumbu Icefall. It's a sobering reminder of the constant danger. They laugh.

Arjun walks over to the puja and says a prayer of thanks, and then Apa does the same. Photos are taken, then Arjun walks over to his tent and sits down on the rocks. Dawa hands him a cellphone and says, "It's your mom."

He blushes as only a young man can, and I turn the camera off for a few minutes and just watch from a distance while he talks to her. When he's off the phone I walk back, camera rolling, and ask him, "So, Arjun, is it what you thought it would be?"

Arjun, now starting to take off his large red boots, responds, "So awesome. As I told you before, it cannot be captured by any camera. It is just what you feel, and you have to be there. It's like, ahhhh. For a few moments you feel like you are at the top of the world, you are the commander, no one is above you. Everyone is below you. It's too good."

I ask him about their journey from Camp Four to the summit.

"We started at 9:30 or 10 p.m., and at that time the moon was quite bright. At the South Summit you see the earth is round. You see the sun coming up, everything slowly started to glow. It's really good."

"When you got to the top were there other people up there?" I ask.

"Yes, yes," he answers. "Loads of people."

Behind me, Apa is still wearing his green climbing helmet, which looks exactly like a bike helmet. Marshall is filming him. I turn my camera on him too.

"I am really glad to be here at Base Camp," he says, and breaks into a big smile, the first relaxed one I've seen. "Safe climb, you know, all the toes and fingers are okay. Now I am ready to go and see my family."

Andrew and I have a quick bite and refresh both cameras with new batteries and new media cards to record on, and I double back to catch up with Marshall. Andrew and I are both going hard. This is our final push near the end of every character's journey. With Apa down he will be leaving soon, maybe tomorrow. There's a hero's welcome awaiting him in Kathmandu. I find Marshall at his tent, packing up. I ask if he thinks there is anything at Base Camp that will have a creeper effect on us when we get home to our domestic lives.

"There are some things that have happened here I am going to have to think about," he replies. "One is the removal of this dead body that just kind of popped up in the middle of Base Camp. It is different to see a dead body here than in Iraq. In Iraq you knew a person had died because another human being killed them, so every time I saw a dead body in Iraq there was this implication about humanity I couldn't avoid. Here, this person died because they were doing what they wanted to do, so it wasn't as disturbing, but then the thought of the body kind of being trapped—I don't know, something about that just really creeped me out and I am going to have to work through that one probably for a while."

"Me too," I say. And then I leave Marshall to finish his packing, thinking about what he said and realizing that I don't fear death as much as I fear how I might die. I think being buried alive would be the most terrifying. I can still see the dead hand reaching out of the frozen glacier, like the hand in the Michelangelo painting in the Sistine Chapel called *The Creation of Adam*, but there the hands are alive and God is reaching back and breathing life into Adam. Here at Base Camp, it's just one lifeless hand reaching up to nothingness, no god reaching back.

Not far away, Dawa is still facing the Khumbu Glacier and shaving with a battery-powered electric shaver while speaking Nepali to someone on the satellite phone. He is pointing at the dozens of people descending the glacier, each looking like a flea on the surface of a large body that could so easily be squashed by the tip of a finger.

Camp is thinning out. As soon as people get down, they get out. No nostalgia for their little community built on rock and ice. Andrew films the packing up, the river of ice-melt that was a mere drip thirty-four days ago, the tilting tents, the fully loaded yaks.

All that is left from the Colombian camp is their stone puja, where a black bird with a yellow beak sits chirping.

Dawa has told us that the monsoon is starting to be active, which is about a week ahead of schedule. It won't affect the climbers but it could affect everyone trying to fly out of Lukla. If it is overcast at all, if there is any kind of precipitation, they shut down the airport. People could get stuck for a week or more.

It has started snowing big time—large flakes. There's a big storm predicted in the next few days. I make a note to pull out my rain pants and raincoat for the hike out. This snow will be rain when we start our descent.

Andrew and I have been feeling a bit off, and now I think he is definitely coming down with something. He's not sleeping, has a bad appetite and is losing weight fast. He has agreed to start taking antibiotics, a three-day dose. I want him to be well on the hike. The water quality is starting to suck. It has a yellow hue and even after boiling tastes off. That could well be the problem.

I've really got to wrap this up and cruise. It looks like we will fall short of forty days: there's the snow, Andrew getting sick and the fact that our characters are almost all down. We will leave as soon as we know whether Rob makes the summit or not. I have spent the night making a list of pros and cons for leaving and decided the only reason not to leave is because my goal was forty days. But actually my goal was a climbing season, which we did. And forty days on the mountain is a metaphor for dropping out and soul searching. And tick, that happened, too. Base Camp has been more soul destruction than soul searching. But I guess things have to fall apart before they can be put back together again. Enlightenment, like the lofty peak of Everest, looks so good from a distance. Clean and pristine, it fills you with the exaltation of a church choir. But what you are looking at is the end, not the journey to get there.

And the journey can be messy.

LESSONS IN HUMILITY

❧

DAY 36: MAY 25

More crazy dreams. I'm on a secret island, covertly swimming in a pool with walls that have caves to hide in. Then I'm in a church sitting next to a guy with a Latina wife who is jealous of me speaking to her husband.

From there, I find myself on my plot of raw land, 4 acres of BC coastal rainforest. I am helping a friend take down some big trees to open the property to more light. In my dream there's a crazy woman living in the forest next to the small clear-cut. She has the ability to shape wood just by touching it. Her home, her things, all made and shaped by her thoughts. She tells me I will regret taking the trees down. In my dreams the clear-cut is way bigger than it actually is, much to my relief as I wake to the biggest snowfall yet and no sun. My tent is buried in snow, and more snow is expected tomorrow. It will be easy to get hurt moving around camp with all the crevasses and hidden glacial streams.

Meagan should come off the mountain today. I've got to check with John to see if Rob summited. He should have gone with John and Darrell. Three days and nights at Camp Four is a long time to spend in the death zone. Maybe the peak is above the storm.

At 9 a.m. I find Comms John looking melancholic in his mess tent. Rob is still in Camp Four. He's kicking himself for not going solo when he arrived there days ago. They are supposed to leave tonight at 7 p.m., but the weather has been crap all day. "Stuff went sideways," he says. "I think the cyclone that was supposed to miss us is overhead right now. If this weather doesn't clear up, we are done, unfortunately."

I nod in sympathy. People don't like to spend one night at Camp

Four. Rob has spent three days there. They call it the death zone for a reason; even on oxygen he is dying up there.

"The guys are all there together now. John and Darrell arrived yesterday morning at 11:30. They all rested, and it looked like it was going to be good. Unfortunately a storm blew in yesterday afternoon, caught some people coming down from the summit, gave some people some scares. The original plan was to go at 7:30, and they made the decision to wait until 9 to see if the weather was just going to blow over but it didn't. It hit the whole mountain from top to bottom."

Apparently some teams left the South Col yesterday around 9 p.m. and all returned before reaching the summit. Comms John says he's been having really spotty radio reception because of clouds, but this morning he heard from Guide John that they were able to get some extra food and fuel from other climbers going down after their summit.

It's quite the juxtaposition: some people stealing oxygen, others sharing their resources. It's an odd little community of thieves and benefactors.

After having some tea with John, Andrew and I head back to Asian Trekking to interview Apa. The snow is coming down hard, so Apa sits just inside the door of his tent. I throw a lavaliere mic on him and we get final comments on the climb.

"It was good. We had clear skies at the summit. Other members go to Camp One, Camp Two, Camp Three and then the summit. I just went from Base Camp straight to Camp Two, then Camp Two straight to the summit and back to Camp Two, then down. I stop at Camp Four for a rest. I used to leave Camp Four with my clients at 9 p.m. but got to the summit too early and too cold to take pictures. So this time I left Camp Four at 12:20, my latest summit push. When I got to the summit I spent two hours on the top taking pictures for my sponsors."

I ask Apa, with people coming from around the world to climb Everest, does he think the mountain can still teach them something?

"Yes, yes," he says. "The mountain teaches the mountaineers how important the weather conditions are, ha ha ha! And it teaches about our own conditions. Good to have experience when climbing. Life is more important, safety first. Every time I'm telling people, life more important.

"And I'm still learning how to help Nepal. This is my number twenty summit. It is very important to me, number twenty. Everest made me famous, so now I am trying to help Nepal. We need our mountain clean."

"Well, you are a cool guy, Apa," I tell him. "And with fame comes responsibility. I respect that you take that seriously." Then jokingly I add, "And you are a handsome guy. Good thing you are married."

I leave him laughing.

The snow is still falling thick and fast. Visibility is horrible, maybe 15 metres. The rest of the team arrives, including Meagan. They all managed to sneak in their summits just before the weather turned. They all had great views.

As I head back to my mess tent I find Chunu standing outside in heavy falling snow, looking up at the glacier. She tells me there has been an accident on the mountain. Word is out on the radio and a small gathering of gear and manpower from various teams is coming together at the base of the glacier.

"At Camp One someone fell in a crack, in a crevasse, hurt back, lots of blood. Hopefully rescue will go good because weather is not so good," Chunu says. Dr. Eric from the HRA walks by with a pack on. It looks like he will be climbing up. I follow him to the base of the glacier where there is a small group of people offering to help with the rescue, most of them guides with other climbing companies who have already gotten their clients safely off the mountain. I film them checking their ropes, putting on their crampons, and agreeing on a radio frequency to communicate on.

Dr. Eric is packed up and getting ready to head up the Khumbu Glacier with two Sherpas. I ask if he has any updates on the condition of the injured climber.

"Not right now," he says. "Information is pretty spotty. Hopefully we will clarify a little bit, sounds like from preliminary reports it is pretty serious. We will see when we get there."

After I film the doctor and the Sherpas walking into the Icefall I head back to the Asian Trekking tent, where I film Dawa on the phone listening to a woman from one of the other teams on the radio. They are discussing how best to help the fallen climber. "A couple of our guys are getting ready to go down to the victim. Sounds like she is near the triple ladders near the top of the Icefall, over," the woman says.

"Aye, copy, triple ladders at the top of the Icefall, yeah," replies Dawa.

Over the phone I can hear the woman saying the Icefall is splitting up and they need help putting ladders in and fixing the route.

"Copy that," Dawa answers. "Right now you need some Sherpas coming from above. Right now our Sherpas just came from South Col and Camp Three. They are pretty tired, I may have a couple, I don't know. But I definitely have Sherpa support here at Base Camp."

As they work out the logistics of support, I look out. Wet snow is coming down hard. I head quickly to our mess tent for fresh camera batteries and to get Andrew to go to the HRA tent to film the progress of the rescue from there. Then I quickly head back to Asian Trekking's communication tent and bump into Bags. It's the first time I have seen her since she abandoned her summit attempt between camps Two and Three. I give her a hug, turn on my camera, try to stabilize it on my shoulder and then ask her what went wrong.

"I left on the morning of May 18, my mom's birthday. My action plan for the summit was between the twenty-seventh and twenty-ninth, and I told Dawa I wanted to make it as soon as possible and rush to Mumbai. That is the mistake that I did. I tried to rush with the team and my body did not acclimatize. I almost made it to Camp Three, but I was very slow. Especially first two days, suffering from high-altitude. I didn't even know what high-altitude is and I got it up there for the first time. I was just murmuring something rubbish. I didn't even remember my name, my mom's name."

I ask Bags if the mountain has taught her anything.

"Yes, absolutely, it did," she says. "Everything my family had went into this expedition. My house, my mom's jewelleries, my grandmother's jewelleries, and the mountain was like, 'Your life is worth more than money.' I wasn't happy when Dawa told me to come down. I realize now it was the right decision." She points to the snow. "Now, I am glad I am not there. That was more than enough for my first summit attempt. I don't look at it like the mountain didn't let me climb her. I see it that she wants me to come back."

After I talk to Bags, I poke my head to check in with Dawa and the rescue up the Icefall. Dawa says it will be a while before there is an update. So I use the time to go and check up on the Canadian team. Of course the busiest part of filmmaking is at the end when you are completely wiped. I'm breathing like I've just been sprinting but I'm walking like a turtle.

I find Comms John sitting all alone in his dining tent with his radio, still looking sad, waiting to hear if the guys will go tonight. "It's frustrating," he says. "It's heartbreaking. Rob had an opportunity to go. Looking back on it I still think he made the right choice in waiting. Having an experienced guide with you is really important on this mountain. And with the weather forecasts we had… I am not going to criticize his decision. I think he made the right decision but it is heartbreaking because he could have summited."

"We will see what happens tonight, I guess."

John crosses his fingers and holds back tears. We sip tea quietly for a few minutes, then he says, "We had six bottles of oxygen stolen from us. Altitude Junkies had oxygen stolen from them. There was a lot of thieving going on before these teams went up. Either steal the summit or kill somebody."

Comms John grabs the satellite phone and goes outside, where it is still snowing heavily. He points it in every direction trying to get through to Camp Four for an update.

"Camp Four from Base Camp?" He tries unsuccessfully for a few minutes and turns to me. "Story of the last twenty-four hours. It has been bad, bad, can't get through."

A few minutes later there is some static on the phone and Guide John's voice comes crackling through. "Okay, we have got everything sorted out. We have enough oxygen to take us up and down in safety, we are going up tonight at 7 p.m., hopefully."

"How's the weather up there?" Comms John asks.

"The wind has died off. Lightly snowing, but pleasant."

"That's good news. It is absolutely puking snow at Base Camp right now so hopefully everything is moving low and you guys will get some decent weather up high."

"Okay, will keep you updated, John out."

MEAGAN

Andrew and I rendezvous at the dining tent where we meet Meagan for a short postclimb interview. The snow has stopped falling, but the skies are still overcast. Meagan has a severe windburn on her cheeks; they look a healthy red but will start peeling within a day. Her hands are dry and chapped. She has already phoned her mom to tell her she is alive and well after summiting Lhotse.

I ask her what she learned on the mountain.

"Well, this time I learned on the mountain the impact that staying at high-altitude can have. By that I mean being over 7,600 metres on no oxygen. I experienced heavy exertion for four days without supplemental oxygen. Even after two days I started experiencing dizziness, even when I was lying down. That has never happened to me before. On oxygen that would not have happened. And yesterday on the summit push [I felt] the physical and mental fatigue of no supplemental oxygen."

I ask her what she thinks the mountain can teach people. Her answer is simple and direct.

"Humility. The mountain can teach humility," she says. "You are a very small organism relative to a huge mass of ice, rock and snow and the spirit force of the mountain. You can be weakened here in the mountains."

Thinking about Rob and the Canadians who have been holed up for days at Camp Four, I ask her how long a person can stay at high-altitudes with oxygen, and what starts to happen to the body.

"When you stay at high-altitude for a while, although you can stay there longer with supplemental oxygen, the body does feel the effects of the altitude. Appetite decreases, and you're probably not drinking as much as you should. Plus one thing to remember is everything at Camp Four is brought up by human power so you only have so much fuel. Your body is wasting away, and your judgment goes as well. And breathing supplemental oxygen is very drying on the lungs so you might develop a bad cough. So when I say you can last a while longer on supplemental oxygen, I mean maybe a couple days, that's about it."

I ask if she experienced a lack of judgment choosing not to go on oxygen for four days at high-altitude.

"That's a good question. Of course it is hard for me to judge, but I think the decisions I made were good because I listened to the guidance of someone who was on supplemental oxygen. I think that's the key, to be with someone who is more coherent than you. So Pemba, my climbing partner, was on supplemental oxygen and I know he has been up Lhotse three times. This was his fourth time, I believe. With his experience with this particular mountain, I listened to his judgment. That is what made everything really successful."

I tell Meagan when I go out into nature, I go there to be by myself. One of the wild things about being here is all the people—thirty-five companies charging anywhere from forty-five to one hundred grand per client. I ask if she thinks commercializing the mountain makes it lose its meaning.

"Yes and no is the easy answer," she says. "I think it depends on the attitude of the person coming. Why are they here? What are their reasons? Are they doing it to conquer something, put another notch in their belt, or are they doing it because they really enjoy the spirit of mountaineering and the challenge that it provides? I think commercialization could be a good thing. It brings more people here to 'share' the beauty of this place. At the same time it could be a bad thing because again you have full lineups on this huge majestic mountain and it kind of takes away from it a little bit. At the same time, it will always be Mt. Everest and you will always have the danger associated with it, and anyone who comes here and steps into the Icefall will have to be humble, and I think that is what is cool about it. You can commercialize the crap out of it but anyone that's up there, the mountain doesn't care who you are, if you are with a commercial expedition or a hard-core, full-on spirited person, you've got to be humble in the mountains."

Arjun is squatting outside his tent, trying to put his crampons back into the torn box they originally came in. The snow has finally stopped falling, and a brief glimpse of sun and blue skies can be seen through the clouds. Weather changes in seconds here.

I tell him, "Dude, I think the box is fried."

"I am just covering them to pack them safe in my bag," he says. "I think I'm leaving tomorrow probably."

"With us?"

"Uh, chopper."

"No, no way."

Arjun smiles. "My father said, 'Why are you wasting time? Come by chopper.' So I said, 'Okay. No problems.'"

"Spoiled guy," I respond in jest.

"What?" He shrugs with a shit-eating grin and ducks back inside his tent to finish packing.

In the evening, the storm breaks, leaving us under cold, clear skies, the silhouette of the mountain crisp in the moonlight. We get an update that the injured climber has been extricated from the crevasse with only minor injuries and will walk down the Khumbu Glacier in the morning. Tomorrow morning we'll get the final report from Comms John about Rob and we'll hit the trail.

Blessed be, I'm going home.

THE DESCENT

We learn this morning that Rob turned around 80 metres from the summit.

John's eyes are red from crying. "Rob is happy," he says. "They sat on the South Col together for thirty minutes. It was pretty apparent when Rob got to the South Summit that he had slowed right down and that he was pretty hammered. He just said, 'I have been through a lot up here and I am okay with this.'"

John starts to cry again. The camera films a few minutes of silence before John continues: "I know on some level he is going to be disappointed, but I think it is going to be short-lived. And I'm fucking proud. I am not feeling disappointed, just a sense of awe and amazement. There have been a lot lesser people that have gone up that mountain and made stupid decisions."

Those are poetic final words on a mountain full of dead people. And their journey parallels mine. We are supposed to stay for another three days but with snow falling and Andrew getting weaker with the alarming amount of weight he is losing, we are leaving today. And my ambition is fried. I'm done, too.

I am also worried about some possible blowback from my disintegrating relationship with Bashista. We need to get back to Kathmandu before him and preferably be landing in Hong Kong by the time he gets there.

This bad weather has also backed things up in Lukla. No flights have been landing or leaving and given that it is the end of the climbing season, there are hundreds waiting to fill those sixteen-seater planes. After a quick breakfast Andrew goes to film the last shot at the Canadian men's tent and I go up to the Asian Trekking dining tent to let everyone know we are hiking out. Meagan, Bags and Marshall are all hiking out tomorrow, and I will see them in Lukla. They are staying at Paradise Lodge with me. We plan on taking Bags out for her first drink in a bar. I ask Meagan to film me doing a small ritual for my friend Delphine, who wanted me to leave a piece of her baby's umbilical cord as an offering to the mountain—a gift of the maiden from the mother to the crone. I say a prayer and tuck it into the puja sitting right at the base of the Khumbu Glacier. Then I say my own thanks and goodbye to the mountain who has been a beautiful goddess, a mean mother and a wise and ancient soul.

There are few other big goodbyes. It will take Miloh and crew two hours to strike and pack up camp. I will see them in Lukla, and that is where I will tip out everybody. Once we got to camp, I spent no money except on a few beers and a dead chicken. I set one thousand dollars aside for a health crisis that I can now use to beef up tips for Miloh and Childon and the porters who will help us descend. The verdict is out on Bashista. All Andrew and I have to do is pack our personal gear and equipment. Most of that is going out on yaks. Everyone else we followed as characters has left except for the Canadian team, whom I know I will see back in Canada. And chances are we are all going to have a few days in Lukla where we will all be waiting for a flight.

Now that the decision is made to leave I am impatient. As I wait for Andrew to finish filming the final beat with John at the Canadian team's tent, I am agitated. I want to go and I don't want to wait. This happened on my visit in 2007, too. I keep trying till I cross the line, and then the shadow kicks in, and I want to tell everybody to just fuck off. I can't wait to be alone. I hate this about myself but then how many people really like their shadow?

Andrew is as eager as I am to start hiking out, but has the grace and patience to get the job done before we go. We film a bit more on our way, then send most of the gear down on porters so that we can enjoy a descent unburdened by the job.

We also agree to go down at our own pace, knowing we will see each other at the end of the day at the lodges. It took us twelve days to hike in with days off for acclimatization. We plan on hiking down to Lukla in three. My muscles have atrophied, I have lost twenty-five pounds and I have put my body and brain through a slow process of oxygen deprivation that I am now going to zap with a huge dose of oxygen. I push hard to get ahead of everybody, put on the iPod for the first time all trip and blast the Talking Heads.

With each step down there is more oxygen. I feel like a dry sponge thrown into water, soaking it in. I have energy and can feel myself coming back to life, literally. The vice grip that bolted into my skull when I arrived has fallen off, and my body feels strong. And I feel so, so happy.

I spend the day hiking by myself and feel the emotional weight of the trip come off my shoulders. The dreams, the weight loss and the introspection played out for everybody there. My summit, the film, was like Rob's. He had to turn back within sight of the peak. I had to turn back within days of my goal.

Our first night we make it to Pheriche, which sits in the valley below the Everest graveyard. It feels great to see goats grazing and potatoes and buckwheat growing in the fields. We have dropped a few thousand metres to 4,370. I am eager to order food from a menu, sit on something resembling a real toilet and have a beer. I am waiting for a private room with a warm shower in Namche tomorrow night.

Sitting next to me in the dining room of the new lodge is a man who lost fingers to frostbite on Everest. He looks Russian but I'm not sure. He also looks to be mourning and I don't want to disturb him with any questions. I have never been to war so I really have no idea what it is like, but I know this experience has been a psychological war zone for me, and looking at the sad face of the man missing his fingers I am guessing for him it is even more so.

On the second day, we hike all the way down to Namche and the first thing I do is have a shower. When I look into the mirror as I'm getting in I realize that the Yeti is actually just a woman who has let herself go. I pluck hairs from my face and chin that are long enough to braid. A year out there and I would look like Leakey's missing link.

A couple of hours later, as my laundry is getting washed, I sit with a cup of tea, recovering from the massage I've just had. I'd booked it with a cousin of the lodge owners, imagining a slow and relaxing rubdown of my body that would release tension from clenched muscles. I imagined the experience would be like every massage I have ever had in my life. The woman walked into my room and put on something that looked like a thick rubber butcher's cape. She said she spoke no English. "That's okay, I'm not into talking, I just want a quiet massage," I thought to myself as I nodded to her. But the rubber butcher's cape had me wondering. She asked me in broken English, "Half hour? Hour?" I said an hour.

I took off my clothes and lay on top of the bed, feeling awkward. Usually I would take off my bra and underwear but left both on. She pointed to the bra. I took that off, leaving the underwear on. She poured cold oil on my legs and belly and roughly rubbed it into my muscles, then started the karate chop—rapid, hard chopping like she was tenderizing meat. For ten minutes I took the pain, thinking, why did I say I wanted an hour? Maybe the karate chop would lead to something gentler. But no—like a chiropractor, without any warning, she flipped me over onto my back, went slap, slap, slap with the oil and karated some more. Now I understood the apron. When she flipped me, she threw my body against her belly to roll me over like a side of beef.

Later that evening, when I walk into the lodge, the owner, the mother, comes over and looks me in the eye. I joke that she must not be my friend for setting me up with a beating instead of a slow and deeply relaxing massage. "You needed to be brought back," she says, and I can see from her face that the beating was meant to be brutal. I was tenderized to make me soft again, to make my spirit soft again. Something that would probably take a dozen beatings at this point.

Bashista and the boys laugh as I hobble in on blistered feet. Their feet are fine as they haven't pushed as hard. They remained calm when I was filled with agitation. Bashista keeps saying, "How was the massage? Haha-

hahah. How was the massage, hahahah?" I laugh with them. I tell them how I paid to get the shit beaten out of me and we all laugh even harder. I love and hate Bashista in this moment.

The next morning I bandage my blistered feet and leave early to avoid hiking with any of my small crew. I just wanted to hobble alone, pretend I am on a masochist's holiday—pain and pleasure, agony and ecstasy, everything one and the same. I grin because I have returned to a land of the living and green fields. I grimace because every step hurts like hell and my body feels like I have been tossed around in an avalanche.

We make it back to Lukla in two days and reconnect with the women from the Asian Trekking gang and the Bad Finns. I get absolutely smashed with Meagan, Bags and some of the other women from Base Camp at a local bar, where we play pool and smoke cigarettes, and the Bad Finns try to get me to snort the salt before I shoot back the tequila. Fortunately, I don't get drunk enough to do that.

The next morning we all have to get up hungover for a flight back to Kathmandu. The small airport is packed with people and bags. One of the Bad Finns is still drinking, obviously going for a three-day bender. He's walking around the airport with the Beach Boys playing on the small cassette player he carries on his shoulder. His friends look like they have actually slept and are now as hungover as the rest of us and embarrassed by their very drunk friend.

As I look around the room of people and bags it seems quite apparent that no matter how many small planes might land today, there will not be enough for everyone here right now. I met people in the lodge yesterday who had gone to the airport three days in a row and still not gotten on a plane. But hours later Andrew, Meagan, Bags and I all receive the go-ahead to board.

Minutes before we get on the plane, I give Miloh and Childon warm hugs and envelopes with generous tips for their service. I give Bashista nothing. Thirty-six days on the mountain have not made me a saint.

When I went to Everest I wondered if there was meaning in what had happened to it over the years. Could all the commercialization and garbage at a mountain revered as a goddess be a microcosm of the larger world, a modern metaphor for human ambition and what we have become?

Remember the old saying, "It's the journey, not the destination"? Well, on Everest it's the destination, not the journey, for many who come with the intention of getting to the top. And perhaps that is true of our society as well. The emphasis is not on process, but on results. We are losing our capacity for patience in a culture built around constantly changing electronic and technological devices that promise faster and faster processing speeds and data transfer. We don't call, we text. We don't hang out, we write on each other's Facebook walls. You would think if we can get men on the moon and a Rover onto Mars we should be able to find a way to ensure clean air, clean water and clean food for all people. You'd think we could also find a way to be sustainable. But instead we think it more important to get to the top, when it should be more important to clean up the bottom. And in this way, Everest is the microcosm of what we're doing to the rest of the world.

HOME

Coming off the plane, I look the same, but lighter. My mother is there with a rose, and standing next to her, my father. But Teresa isn't there. She is at work. My friends have a beer waiting for me in a van. I return to my house, but not to my home. Within days one close friendship dissolves; within months, my marriage.

Every climber carries a photo of their kids or partner in their pocket. I carried the note Teresa gave me for my birthday and reread it daily— something soft in that hard landscape. As I got to know many of the climbers at Base Camp I realized many of them were carrying pictures from relationships and marriages that had failed.

It is hard to love a person who is driven to leave all the time to do dangerous things. The fear, the worry, the financial costs, and for what? What does the person who gets left behind get from the experience? In many cases when the adventurer returns home, it's to someone whose life has continued without them and so they are outsiders in their own lives. I now felt like an outsider in mine.

Andrew's relationship of twelve years fell apart too. Something changed for both of us. Andrew says it was hard to make the relationship work again. He thinks it was the time away without much chance to communicate more than it was the place itself. And he says Base Camp awakened other things in him that he still holds onto.

I had hoped that living in the belly of the great goddess Chomolunga, I would find ancient wisdom. I don't know that I did, but a year later I find these words written by one of Everest's first climbers, and victims, George Mallory, and now I see the wisdom in me.

Have we vanquished an enemy? None but ourselves.
Have we gained success? That word means nothing here.
Have we won a kingdom? No… and yes.
We have achieved an ultimate satisfaction…
fulfilled a destiny… To struggle and to understand—never this last without the other: such is the law…

George Mallory (1911)

PHOTO CAROLINA AHUMADA CALA

AFTERWORD

This memoir is a collage of my personal perceptions of Everest Base Camp and the interviews and conversations I had with other people there. Since reality is an interpretation, these words express my opinion only.

Interviews have been lightly edited for clarity and length.

The film, *40 Days at Base Camp*, has won awards and been in festivals all over the globe. It has been translated into many languages and is currently available on iTunes worldwide. You can find more information about the film at www.40daysatbasecamp.com and about me at www.diannewhelan.com

THANK YOU

My publisher, Vici Johnstone, and the other good people at Caitlin Press, Andrea Routley, Kathleen Fraser and Holly Vestad. Maggie Langrick for her love and help with my first draft. My editor, Jane Silcott, who helped make this a better read. The Minister's wife for pushing the buttons of my soul on the final draft and asking hard questions. My friends Jenica and Kim, my sister, Nicole, and my mom and dad for lighting candles on my darkest days and who accept my shadow with my light. My godchildren Liam, Cole and Marley and to all my dear friends and family— if I list one I have to list you all so you know who you are and I love you. To Andrew Coppin for sharing the experience and shooting beautiful footage. To all the people in this book who shared their stories with me, especially Meagan McGrath, Arjun Vajpai, Nelson Cardona Carvajal and Robert Hill.

And lastly I dedicate this book to Teresa Karbashewski. The mountain is littered with frozen dreams, casualties of Everest. And I am sorry the life we had was one of them.

Blessed be.

DIANNE WHELAN is an award-winning Canadian filmmaker, photographer, author and multimedia artist. In April 2010, Whelan travelled to Nepal and Mount Everest Base Camp to direct and shoot her award-winning documentary film *40 Days at Base Camp*. Whelan's first book, *This Vanishing Land* (Caitlin Press), recalls her experience as an embedded media person on a historical sovereignty patrol in the Canadian High Arctic. Her National Film Board documentary, *This Land*, is based on the same journey. Whelan is currently working on her next film and book project, called *The Story of White Raven*, which weaves the indigenous legend of the white animals into the current war on nature.